THE NEW BIBLE COOKBOOK

God's Food for Thought— Nourishment for the Soul

by

Sue Cameron

For Patricia,
God Bless !
Sue Cameron

To Phoebe Snow
and Joan Rivers

CONTENTS

Acknowledgments xiii

Introduction xv

1. BEGINNINGS

Abundance *Abundance Salad*
with Honey-fruit Dressing 23

Action *Action-Stuffed Mushrooms* 26

Overcoming the Odds
Beating the Odds Spinach Dip 28

Blessing *Blessed Salad* 30

Gladness *Chopped Liver of Gladness* 32

Commitment *Committed Corn Soup* 34

Just Ask *Cottage Cheese Balls for the Asking* 36

Delight *Delightful Bacon Crisps* 38

Your God *God's Easy Bean Barley Soup* 40

Counsel *Soup of Good Counsel* 42

Healing *Healing Lentil Soup* 44

Health *Healthy Manna Bread Soup* 46

Keep Going *Keep Going Soup* 48

Love *Love Salad*.................................. 50

Love Thy Neighbor *Loving Lentil Soup* 52

New Age Health *New Age Matzo Ball Soup* 54

Passion *Passionate Pomegranate Salad*................. 56

Prosperity *Prosperous Soup*.................... 58

Life *Red Soup of Life*............................... 60

Respectable Behavior *Respectful Cheese Puffs*......... 62

Control *Spirit-Controlled Mushroom Salad* 64

Stars *Starry Mushroom Soup with Dumplings* 66

Steadiness *Steady Cheddy Cheese Balls*................. 68

Listen *We Hear You Cucumber Salad*................... 70

2. MIDDLES

Idle Talking *Action Chicken Casserole*..................... 75

Serenity *Anxiety-Free Ribs*........................... 77

Blind Faith *Blindly Hot Chicken Salad*.................. 79

Celebration *Celebrative Lamb Medley*..................... 81

Compassion *Compassionate Couscous*..................... 83

Confidence *Confident Easy Pot Roast*..................... 85

Discernment *Discerning Fruited Meatballs*.............. 87

Dreams vs. Fantasies *Dreamy Ham Loaf*.............. 89

Gifts of Love *Dumplings of Love*..................... 91

Exultation *Exulted Macaroni Salad*..................... 93

Flaming to the Tree of Life

Flaming Filet Mignon.............95

Giving *Gifted Pot Roast* 98

Glory *Glorious Shish Kebabs*..................100

Glory of God *Glow of God Brisket*...........102

Joyful God *God's Joyful Chicken*.............104

Good Things *Good Things Casserole*.......................106

Hard Work *Hard-Working Meatballs*.....................108

Hope *Hopeful Chicken*.................................111

Humility *Humble Salmon Croquettes*...................113

Beginnings *In the Beginning Chicken* 115

Strength *Iron Strength Liver Stroganoff*..............117

Joy *Joyful Lamb Stew*.........................119

Judging *Judgment Beef Casserole*.......................121

Mercy and Love *Lovely Garlic Shrimp* 123

Nighttime *Midnight Mediterranean Pilaf.* 125

Doubt *Never Doubt Corn Ring* 127

Obedience *Obedient Omelet* 129

Order *Orderly Potatoes*................................131

Freedom *Pasta "Free-tata"*.....................................133

Negativity No More *Positive Lamb Chops*................136

Rejoice *Rejoicing Salmon from Habakkuk*................138

Wake Up *Rise 'n' Shine Salmon Loaf*.....................140

Faith and More Faith

Salmon with Faith Mustard.................................. *142*

Satisfaction *Satisfying Dilled Pork*........................ *144*

Seeking *Seekers'Baked Chicken*............................. *146*

Armor of Faith *Shield of Faith Chicken*.................... *148*

Testing of Belief *Tested Filet of Sole*.................... *150*

Truth-Finding

Truthful Game Hen Stuffed with Figs *152*

Truth *Truthful Chicken, Olive and Nut Salad*......... *154*

Comfort *Comforting Macaroni and Cheese* *156*

Wholeness *Wholeness Vegetable Casserole*............... *158*

3. ENDINGS

Belief *Believable Bread Pudding* *163*

Contentment *Contented Cookies*............................ *165*

Diligence *Diligent Shortbread* *167*

Eternity *Eternal Cranberry Velvet*........................ *169*

Conquering Fear *Fearless Scones*.......................... *171*

Harmony *Harmonious Apple Pudding*.................... *173*

Loving Others

Lovingly Baked Caramel Custard *175*

Manual Labor *Laborer's Luscious Lemon* *177*

Perseverance *Persevering Banana Muffins* *179*

Possibilities *Possible Apple Crisp* 181

No Doubts, No Sin *Simply Sinful Chocolate Cake*... 183

Future *Sweet Potato Future Pie* 186

Worship *Worshipful Peach Pleasure* 188

4. ODDS & ENDS

Advice *Advisable Onions au Gratin* 193

Bow Down *Bowing Down Party-Size Egg Salad* 195

Life Patterns *Bread of Life* 197

Giving *Cheerful Giving Bread* 200

Craving *Cravable Potato Pancakes* 202

Don't Despair *Despair-Free Date Nut Bread* 204

Reaping Energy *Energized Potatoes* 206

Faith *Faithful Bread of Life* 208

Following *Followers' Pancakes* 210

The Cycle of Life *Fruit of Life Bread* 212

Gain *Gainful Potatoes* 214

Gathering *Gathering Eggplant* 216

Generosity *Generously Measured Polenta* 218

Grace *Graceful Heaven Cakes* 220

Harvesting *Harvest Corn Pie* 223

Real Faith *Real Faithful Green Rice* 225

Mercy *Merciful Knishes* 227

Freedom of Spirit *Honeyed Apples of Freedom* *229*

True Riches *Rich 'n' Spicy Cashew Nuts* *231*

Reach Out *Reach Out Carrot Ring*.......................*233*

Reward *Rewarding Easy Spinach*.........................*235*

Personal Care *Rice of Care*.................................. *237*

Righteousness *Righteous Mint Relish* *239*

Wisdom *Solomon's Corn Bread*.............................*241*

Heart and Soul *Soulful Blintz Souffle*................... *243*

Success *Successful Egg-Cheese Surprise* *245*

Worry *Worry-Free Applesauce Puffs*.........................*247*

ACKNOWLEDGMENTS

I would like to thank Ronnie Frankel for his thorough research, and I have a feeling he'd like to thank me for his newfound knowledge. I am grateful to his mother, Sandra L. A. F. S. Pressman, and to event planner Shelly Balloon for their recipe consultations and demonstrations.

Further thanks go to the Rev. Durmond Blatnik, for our many shared thoughts and conversations about the Bible and his recommendations for citations.

INTRODUCTION

Food for Thought
or
Nourishment for the Soul

God blessed them, saying to them, "Be fruitful, multiply, fill the earth and conquer it. Be masters of the fish of the sea, the birds of heaven and all living animals on the earth." God said, "See, I give you all the seed-bearing plants that are upon the whole earth, and all the trees with seed-bearing fruit; this shall be your food. To all wild beasts, all birds of heaven and all living reptiles on the earth I give all the foliage of plants for food." And so it was.

Genesis 1:28-50

I live in Los Angeles, California, right in the middle of earthquakes, fires, floods, mud slides, scandals and murder. It is difficult to achieve a balanced or harmonious life here. You must fight for it, to take the time for yourself, to create a special world that is healthy. Making a world for yourself, no matter where you live, is essential. We all have problems and stress, regardless of where we live or what we do for a living.

What we put into our minds, the sounds we allow our ears to hear, the sights we give to our eyes, and the food we put into our bodies all are important. We can try to control things, but it is impossible to escape today's trash. Just the local news can make me feel nervous.

My parents raised me to respect all people and all religions. They told me that if someone displayed a good value system and tried to live a decent life, that person deserved my respect. Almost all religions try to encourage us to be our best. For many years I have studied everything from Christianity to Taoism and I am fascinated by all of it. My initial interest at some point turned to a way of life. I love reading the Bible. I like to read it every morning for about 15 minutes. Sometimes I just open the book at random, feeling that God is guiding my fingers to verses for me to read that day. Other times I go to Proverbs or Psalms and pick out the verse that corresponds with the particular date of that morning. Every day I get this special learning experience and it makes me feel better. I am grounded, prepared and ready to start the day.

One of my other passions, besides religion, is food. My grandparents lived across the street from

me when I was growing up. Grandma Cameron was born in Hawaii and married my grandfather when he was stationed there during one of the wars. They eventually moved to Los Angeles, and some of my fondest memories are of Grandma's home-cooked meals every day after school. She and Grandpa ate around four in the afternoon, and that was perfect for me. We had exotic dishes of Spanish rice, comforting meals of meatballs, gravy and mashed potatoes, incredible macaroni and cheese, and wonderful pies made from scratch. To this day I still get hungry every day at four o'clock because of my grandparents.

My parents, on the other hand, were very sophisticated people. They took me out each week to a different restaurant to educate me about tastes and food.

By the time I was 10 I was craving sukiyaki, lemon chicken, goulash, French vegetable soup, Welsh rarebit, smoked salmon, and kreplach. I could tell you which restaurant had a better chocolate souffle. I would spit out instant mashed potatoes if, God forbid, I discovered them on my plate. I liked to add sherry wine to my tomato or split pea soup. I was no ordinary kid, and I grew up loving and appreciating all kinds of food.

Today I am still obsessed with food. It gives me great joy. I am lucky in that I don't need to gorge myself or eat all of something. Having a taste makes me happy, but it had better be the right taste that I crave, at exactly the right time. I may be craving a cheeseburger, but do I want a sloppy one, a chic one, a plain bun, a homemade cheese bun-—it just goes on and on. I derive great joy from making each culinary choice. When I travel, one of the first places I like to go is the local market. I'll be there forever. As souvenirs I bring home jars of condiments and bread mixes. Forget the T-shirts, I'd rather have a special relish.

I meet with master chefs all the time, too. I once even flew to France for dinner! I took a flight from Los Angeles to Paris, then a connecting one from Paris to Nice. I rented a car and drove to the village of St. Paul de Vence to keep a reservation at a restaurant called La Colombe d'Or. I was only 10 minutes late, and it was the greatest dining adventure I've ever had. To me, each meal, each bite, is a treasure. I feel better when I have a good meal. I'd rather not eat than eat something mediocre.

Food and religion may seem far apart to you, but to me they are not. Food is Life. God is Life. He created all food, didn't He? Once I made the connection, I started looking in the Bible to see exactly what foods it mentioned. It took over a year, just finding the foods and playing with the ingredients. Then it hit me. If I can put God's words into my head, why not put the food into my stomach? That way I'll be healthy in every area. And so *The Bible Cookbook* was born. I have so enjoyed marrying God's thoughts to his food. Writing this book has made my face smile, my stomach gurgle with delight, and my mind contemplate his words. I have built a complete defense system against the bad onslaughts of life. With some nourishing thoughts, some nourishing food, I have a better life, and now you can, too. These recipes are clear and simple, just the way God should be. Cooking should be fun and not frightening. This is pure, homey, comforting food. If you're looking for arugula or a ganache, you won't find it here.

I celebrate God every day with beautiful thoughts and pure food right from the Bible. Cleanse your body, mind and soul by gathering into your physical being only those words, thoughts and ingredients created by the Supreme Being.

Think of his words and as you cook and eat, let your mind wander back to ancient times when all our ancestors honored God as they ate.

All recipes serve four, unless otherwise indicated.

BEGINNINGS

BEGINNINGS

Abundance

*Nevertheless, I will bring health and healing
to it; I will heal my people and will let them enjoy
abundant peace and security.*

Jer. 55:6

Open your eyes and look around. God's abundance is everywhere. We are surrounded by his gifts. Feel good about yourself because that's what he wants. Take it all in: the air, the smells, the colors, and be happy today. He has blessed us!

BEGINNINGS

Abundance Salad

3/4 cup couscous

1/2 cup raisins

3 dates, chopped

1/2 apple, diced

Dash of vinegar

1/2 cup pistachios,

chopped

1/4 teaspoon cinnamon

1 cup grapes

1 cup melon, chopped

1/2 cup figs

Lettuce leaves for garnish

Prepare couscous as directed on box and let cool. Add all other ingredients except for melon, figs and lettuce. Form mounds of couscous by placing in small cup, pressing it and quickly turning upside down on a bed of lettuce. Place extra grapes and pieces of melon and figs in a ring around the couscous.

BEGINNINGS

Honey-Fruit Dressing

1 melon, cut   *2 tablespoons oil*

1/2 cup honey   *1/4 teaspoon salt*

Liquify melon in blender. Mix in honey, oil and salt.

BEGINNINGS

Action

In the same way, faith by itself, if it is not accompanied by action, is dead.

James 2:17

You can believe all you want, but if you don't do anything about it, having faith is pointless. Don't waste your life. Do something. Dare to make a few mistakes. Doing nothing is the worst mistake—but think first!

BEGINNINGS

Action-Stuffed Mushrooms

1 pound mushrooms	*1/2 teaspoon*
with stems and caps	*Worcestershire sauce*
1 tablespoon onion,	*1/4teaspoon salt*
minced	*6 slices bacon,*
1/4 cup butter, melted	*cooked and crumbled*
1 tablespoon parsley,	*1 tablespoon plus*
minced	*1 teaspoon Parmesan*
1/3 to 1/2 cup seasoned	*cheese, grated*
bread crumbs	*1 cup cream*

Lightly grease shallow baking pan. Clean mushrooms, remove stems and chop stems finely. Cook stems and onion slowly in butter for five minutes. Add next seven ingredients and toss lightly. Fill mushroom caps with this mixture and place in dish. Sprinkle with Parmesan cheese. Bake at 400° for 15 to 20 minutes.

BEGINNINGS

Overcoming the Odds

I have told you these things, so that in me you may have peace. In this world you will have trouble. But take heart! I have overcome the world.

John 16:53

God gave you the ability to overcome. Nothing worthwhile is easy. *When* you think you can't, call on God to give you the wisdom and strength you need to win.

BEGINNINGS

Beating the Odds
Spinach Dip

1 package frozen
  spinach, thawed,
  drained and
  squeezed
1/2 cup parsley,chopped
1/2 cup green onion,
  chopped

1/2 teaspoon dill
1 teaspoon seasoned
  salt
1 cup mayonnaise
1 cup sour cream
Juice of 1/2 lemon

Mix all ingredients and refrigerate. Make this dip the day before you plan to serve. Excellent with raw vegetables.

BEGINNINGS

Blessing

Blessed are those who have learned to acclaim you, who walk in the light of your presence, 0 Lord.

Ps. 89:15

Today I will bless everyone I see. I feel completely safe, knowing that God blesses me. Everyone needs to feel God's blessing. Even if I dislike how someone acts, I will bless that person with kindness and compassion. I feel God's peace and share it freely. God is taking care of me and my house. I am his servant.

BEGINNINGS

Blessed Salad

1/2 cup heavy whipping cream	*1 small apple, shredded*
1 clove garlic, crushed	*1/2 cup raisins*
2 cups cabbage, shredded	*1 small can black, olives*
2 cups lettuce, shredded	*1/4 teaspoon salt*

Whip cream and add crushed garlic. Place cabbage, lettuce, apple and raisins in a bowl. Fold in whipped cream and garlic mixture. Place on a lettuce leaf and slice olives on top. Salt to taste.

BEGINNINGS

Gladness

The meadows are covered with flocks and the valleys are mantled with grain; they shout for joy and sing.

Ps. 65:13

Imagine floating in a pool of still water. Feel its coolness against your skin. Beneath you imagine a spring of water, bubbling from deep within the earth, caressing you as it streams to the surface. Joy is like that, welling up from the depths of our spirit, refreshing and reviving us. Wait for joy to rise to the surface of your consciousness. Let it pour through you to everyone around you today.

BEGINNINGS

Chopped Liver of Gladness

1 onion, chopped   *2 hard-boiled eggs*

3 tablespoons chicken fat   *Salt, paprika and pepper*

1 pound chicken livers   *to taste*

Saute onions in chicken fat. Remove from pan and place in mixing bowl. Cook liver in the same pan until well done. Remove and add to bowl. Chop eggs and add them, mixing everything together. Add salt, pepper and paprika to taste.

BEGINNINGS

Commitment

Commit to the Lord whatever you do, and your plans will succeed.

Prov. 16:3

Once you have committed yourself to God, you may succeed at giving yourself for life to another person. If God comes first in both your lives, your common commitment will cement your relationship to each other. God will watch over both of you, strengthen the bond of love between you, and guide you safely through occasional storms into peaceful waters.

BEGINNINGS

Committed Corn Soup

1 large onion, chopped

2 pats butter

1 quart milk

*2 cups shredded
    cheddar cheese*

2 cups fresh corn

1/4 teaspoon honey

1/4 teaspoon pepper

1/4 teaspoon dry mustard

1/4 teaspoon cumin

1/2 teaspoon salt

In a saucepan saute onion in butter until clear. Add milk, cheese, corn and other ingredients. Bring to a boil, cover and simmer for 20 minutes.

BEGINNINGS

Just Ask

Do not be anxious about anything, but in everything, by prayer and petition, with thanksgiving, present your requests to God.

Phil. 4:6

God will always listen. Feel free to pray about anything, no matter what it is. Trust God to answer. He may say no to your request, but always says yes to you. He created you, loves you and plans only good for you.

BEGINNINGS

Cottage Cheese Balls for the Asking

2 cups cottage cheese

2 tablespoons milk
or cream

1/4 cup pecans, chopped

1/4 cup parsley, chopped

Cream cottage cheese and milk together to make a paste. Roll into balls and roll these in nuts and parsley. Chill. Serve very cold.

BEGINNINGS

Delight

*Delight yourself in the Lord and he will give
you the desires of your heart.*

Ps. 57:4

The more you get to know God and his will for you, the more delight you will discover. As you begin to want what God wants for you, joy fills your heart. When you truly love God with all your heart, soul, mind and strength, and your neighbor as yourself— then you can do as you please because you want, most of all, to please God.

BEGINNINGS

Delightful Bacon Crisps

Wrap a single cracker of your choice with a slice of uncooked bacon. Make as many as you wish and place them on a cookie sheet. Bake at 550° for 15 minutes. Drain on a paper towel and serve.

BEGINNINGS

Your God

Where can I go from your Spirit? Where can I flee, from your presence? If I go up to the heavens, you are there; if I make my bed in the depths, you are there. If I rise on the wings of the dawn, if I settle on the far side of the sea, even there your hand will guide me, your right hand will hold me fast.

Ps. 159:7-10

You belong to God. He is always with you, whether you are in a house of worship, in a mountain meadow or in your kitchen. He gives himself to you because he loves you, just as he loves all creation. Whatever you think, say or do, let who you are today flow from God.

BEGINNINGS

God's Easy Bean Barley Soup

1/2 cup barley	*3 stalks celery, chopped*
2 quarts water	*Impounds meaty soup*
1 cup lima beans	*bones*
1/2 cup navy beans	*4 carrots, sliced*
1 onion, chopped	*Salt and pepper to taste*

Place all ingredients in a heavy pot and cook, covered, over low flame for 2 to 5 hours.

BEGINNINGS

Counsel

You guide me with your counsel, and afterward you will take me into glory.

Ps. 75:24

If we listen to God and His counsel, and if we practice what we learn, we will go to heaven. It's as simple as that. And if we help others to learn what we have learned, we will be doing God's work and letting more people into heaven, and they in turn will be working and teaching more people. This is the Word of God.

If we listen to God and His counsel, and practice what we learn, we begin to experience heaven here on earth. Heaven in this life and the next is where God reigns. Teaching others what we've learned is God's work. We can invite them to open their hearts to God's presence, as we have.

BEGINNINGS

Soup of Good Counsel

1/3 rasher of bacon	*1 cup barley*
(3 slices)	*2 tablespoons parsley*
2 tablespoons olive oil	*1/2 cup red wine*
2 large onions, chopped	*4 teaspoons sour cream*
1 teaspoon garlic	*2 quarts beef stock*

Cook bacon in a pan. Drain, crumble and set aside. Saute chopped onions and garlic in olive oil in a pot. Add beef stock to pot. Boil barley separately, drain and set aside. Add parsley to boiling broth. Add bacon, barley and red wine; simmer for 10 minutes. Serve with a dollop of sour cream in each bowl.

BEGINNINGS

Healing

Do not be wise in your own eyes; fear the Lord and shun evil. This will bring health to your body and nourishment to your bones.

Prov. 5:7-8

Our bodies are temples of life. When God's love flows through us, we feel secure, peaceful and healthy. Eating healthy foods, as God wants you to, will contribute to your staying fit and trim. Just as God provides food for the body, so He also gives nourishment for the soul. Both body and spirit experience wholeness and healing.

BEGINNINGS

Healing Lentil Soup

3 garlic cloves,
chopped

2 onions, chopped

2 tablespoons olive oil

1/2 cups lentils

3 ribs celery

1 cup vegetable stock

1 quart water or white
wine

Salt and pepper to taste

2 tablespoons parsley,
chopped

2 teaspoons fresh lemon
juice

Saute garlic and onions in olive oil in a stock pot
Add lentils, celery, stock and water. Bring to a boil;
add salt and pepper to taste, parsley and lemon juice.
Bring back to a slow boil for 40 minutes. Serve as
soup or over rice.

BEGINNINGS

Health

You are to worship your God, and I shall bless your bread and water, and remove sickness from among you.

Exod. 25:25

God has a plan for your life. When you live by faith, not by sight, you live fully. Whether you are physically sick or well, God wants you to be spiritually whole. Some persons coping with chronic illness teach the rest of us how to live to the fullest. From God comes the food that nourishes our bodies, and the faith that transcends them.

BEGINNINGS

Healthy Manna Bread Soup

4 tablespoons butter	*1 medium size onion,*
6 slices large grain	*chopped*
bread	*6 cups chicken broth*
6 tablespoons plain flour	*Salt and pepper to taste*

Melt one tablespoon of butter and brush over bread. Cut bread into cubes and place on foil-lined baking sheet. Toast in 400° oven until brown. Melt remaining butter in saucepan. Stir in flour and onion, and cook over moderate heat until dark. Stir in broth a little at a time and bring to boil. Add salt and pepper; simmer for 50 minutes. Add bread cubes to bowls and serve.

BEGINNINGS

Keep Going

Where a man sows, there he reaps: if he sows in the field of self-indulgence he will get a harvest of corruption out of it; if he sows in the field of the Spirit he will get from it a harvest of eternal life.

Gal. 6:7-8

You reap what you sow. If you work in God's field, you'll harvest a rich blessing. Don't be distracted. Work hard. Keep at it. God will bless you every day. Goodness is its own reward, now and in eternity.

BEGINNINGS

Keep Going Soup

1 cup onion, cubed	3 tablespoons unbleached
1/4 cups leek, cut	wheat flour
4 tablespoons butter	1 teaspoon ground
2 cups chicken broth	coriander
1 pint half-and-half	% teaspoon cumin
1/4 stick butter	Salt to taste
	Parsley as garnish

Saute separately onion and leek, each in two tablespoons butter. Add both to chicken broth in saucepan, then add half-and-half. Cook at medium temperature. Mix V4 stick butter and flour to creamy consistency and add to soup while heating. Add coriander and cumin, and salt to taste. Sprinkle chopped parsley on top and serve.

BEGINNINGS

Love

The fig tree is forming its first figs and the blossoming vines give out their fragrance. Come then, my love, my lovely one, come. My dove, hiding in the clefts of the rock, in the coverts of the cliff, show me your face, let me hear your voice; for your voice is sweet and your face is beautiful.

Song 2:15-14

Love of God is paramount, above all things. Through this love we can love each other and all life. Concentrate on loving others. Today someone needs to know that you love him. Make him feel good. Your love will return to you.

BEGINNINGS

Love Salad

2 cantaloupes	3/4 cup watermelon
2 pomegranates,	3/4 cup raisins
3/4 cup honey dew melon	3/4 cup chopped figs
1 cup grapes, halved	3/4 cup date meat
and seeded	Mint for garnish

For dressing:

1 cup sour cream	1/2 teaspoon cinnamon
3 tablespoons honey	

Make melon baskets by cutting two cantaloupes in half and use a melon baller to take out meat. Cut jagged edges on side of basket to garnish melon. Mix all the fruits together in bowl and then transfer to melon halves. Serve with chilled sour cream dressing. Use mint for garnish.

BEGINNINGS

Love Thy Neighbor

My brothers, you were called, as you know, to liberty; but be careful, or this liberty will provide an opening for self-indulgence. Serve one another, rather, in works of love, since the whole of the Law is summarized in a single command: Love our neighbor as yourself.

Gal. 5:15-14

We often say, "Love thy neighbor." But God wishes us to put this saying into practice. How long has it been since you have done something nice for your neighbor? Start today by making two dishes of this recipe. Keep one for yourself and take one next door. Better yet, share the meal with your neighbor if he or she is alone, and put your dish in the freezer.

BEGINNINGS

Losing Lentil Soup

2 cups dry lentils,
  soaked and washed
7 cups chicken bouillon
1/2 cups chicken,
  cooked and shredded
1 large onion, chopped

1 medium leek
4 tablespoons oil
Salt to taste
1 tablespoon wine
  vinegar
1/3 cup cooked barley
  or oats

Cook lentils in water until moisture is absorbed. Add chicken bouillon and cooked chicken meat. Saute onion and leek in oil and add to soup. Add salt, 'vinegar and grain. Cook for 1 hour over low heat.

BEGINNINGS

New Age Health

When evening came, many who were demon
possessed were brought to him, and he drove out
the spirits with a word and healed all the sick.

Matt. 8:16

As a child of God, I know that the first step toward getting healthy is prayer. I can practice both Western and Eastern medicine in combination. Yet I know in my heart that my health conies from the life force of God. I can pray alone or with others. I will concentrate on believing that I will be healthy. I trust in God.

BEGINNINGS

New Age Matzo Ball Soup

3 eggs

1/4 cup heated chicken
  fat

1/2 cup matzo meal

1/2 cup parsley, chopped

1 teaspoon salt

4 12-ounce cans
  chicken broth

2 large onions, chopped

For matzo balls:

Mix eggs, chicken fat, and matzo meal. Refrigerate.

For soup:

Bring salted water to boil. Make the matzo mixture into balls and add to water. Boil, covered, for 25 to 55 minutes. Add broth, onions and parsley, and simmer for 45 minutes.

BEGINNINGS

Passion

How delicious is your love, more delicious than wine! How fragrant your perfumes, more fragrant than all other spices! Your lips, my promised one, distill wild honey.

Song 4:10-11

Obeying God does not mean a life without passion. He gives us our emotions and rejoices in our happiness. Giving oneself freely, totally, to another is part of God's plan. You have been given the gift of judgment and will love wisely. God wants us to experience love, passion and commitment. Do so in His name.

BEGINNINGS

Passionate Pomegranate Salad

1 head romaine lettuce	*1 small can black*
2 chicken breasts, grilled	*olives*
1/2 cup goat cheese	*2 pomegranates*

For dressing (per person):

2 parts oil	*1 teaspoon honey*
1 part rose vinegar	

On a bed of lettuce, shred the grilled chicken, topping with crumbled goat cheese and sliced olives. Sprinkle buds of pomegranates on top and add dressing.

BEGINNINGS

Prosperity

He is like a tree planted by streams of water,
which yields its fruit in season and whose leaf
does not winter. Whatever he does prospers.

Ps. 1:5

God wants us to use all His gifts and teachings. When we faithfully obey His laws and use His gifts, we become rich spiritually and sometimes materially as well. Follow God's teachings and make the most of His gifts. Your hard work will make your dreams of prosperity come true. God deserves nothing less, and neither do you.

BEGINNINGS

Prosperous Soup

Pinch of cinnamon	*Pinch of salt*
Pinch of nutmeg	*1/2 cup sweet white wine*
1 tablespoon honey	*6 cups chicken broth*
6 egg yolks	*3 tablespoons butter*

Mix cinnamon, nutmeg and honey in separate bowl and reserve. Beat egg yolks in saucepan; add salt, wine and broth. Stir in butter and keep stirring on medium heat until mixture thickens. Do not boil. Pour in soup bowls and sprinkle with topping that you reserved.

BEGINNINGS

Life

/ tell you most solemnly, it was not Moses who gave you bread from heaven, it is my Father who gives you the bread from heaven, the true bread; for the bread of God is that which comes down from heaven and gives life to the world. I am the bread of life. He who comes to me will never be hungry; he who believes in me will never thirst.

John 6:48

God is life and life is God. God is ageless and eternal. I believe that no matter what happens to my flesh, I am eternal with him. Knowing that allows me to live each day to the fullest, free from fear. I feel protected every moment. That gives me strength to be the best person I can. I am going to concentrate on being my best every minute today.

BEGINNINGS

Red Soup of Life

2 cans kidney beans	*3 tablespoons wheat flour*
1/2 cup cream	*1/2 garlic clove*
4 cups chicken broth	*1 teaspoon salt*
1/2 stick warm butter	*5 tablespoons chopped parsley*

Mix in blender two cans of beans with cream. Place ½ bean mixture in saucepan. Add broth and warm over medium heat. Stir together butter, flour, and garlic to a creamy consistency; then add to saucepan with beans. Add salt and simmer for 10 minutes with remaining beans added. Sprinkle chopped parsley on top for color and taste, and serve.

BEGINNINGS

Respectable Behavior

Let us behave decently, as in the daytime, not in orgies and drunkenness, not in sexual immorality and debauchery, not in dissension and jealousy.

Rom. 15:13

Honor God and yourself with your behavior. No one wants to be a prude, but some behavior is tacky, inappropriate, unnecessary and crude. Never act like that. Always behave properly, no matter how hard it is. We want the respect of God, and just as important, we want to respect ourselves. If we don't respect ourselves, who will?

BEGINNINGS

Respectful Cheese Puffs

1 cup sharp cheddar
   cheese, grated
3 tablespoons soft butter
1/2 cup flour, sifted

1/4 teaspoon salt
1/4 teaspoon paprika
1 small jar stuffed green
   olives

Blend cheese and butter. Stir in flour, salt and paprika. Roll mixture by hand around olives and place on ungreased cookie sheets. Bake at 400° for 10 to 15 minutes. Makes 50 or more puffs.

BEGINNINGS

Control

The mind of sinful man is death, but the mind controlled by the Spirit is life and peace.

Rom. 8:6

Control can be good or bad. You choose. Never try to control people with an ego game. But you have control over your life, if you keep your behavior in check and bad images out of your mind. To control yourself with manners, discipline and restraint is very good. Let God's Spirit control you. God's control always has positive results for you.

BEGINNINGS

Spirit-Controlled Mushroom Salad

*10 small whole mush-
room caps, not stems*

1/4 cup salad oil

1/4 cup cider vinegar

*1 tablespoon onion,
finely chopped*

*1 tablespoon parsley,
finely chopped*

1 clove garlic, crushed

1/4 teaspoon salt

1/4 teaspoon sugar

Lettuce for garnish

Watercress for garnish

Wash mushrooms and remove stems. Combine other ingredients (except lettuce and watercress) for marinade. Add washed mushrooms, cover and refrigerate overnight. Serve on lettuce and watercress as a salad.

BEGINNINGS

Stars

Lift your eyes and look to the heavens: Who created all these? He who brings out the starry host one by one, and calls them each by name. Because of his great power and mighty strength, not one of them is missing.

Isa. 40:26

Just as stars light the heavens, stars shine on the earth. We all are stars. The same God who governs the celestial stars takes care of us, too. You may sometimes feel like a small speck in the universe. But you aren't—just as the stars only appear to be tiny pinpricks of light. We are God's stars.

BEGINNINGS

Starry Mushroom Soup with Dumplings

For soup:

1/8 pound butter	*2 thick slices onion*
2 tablespoons flour	*1 tablespoon paprika*
1 cup mushrooms,	*1/2 quarts water*
	sliced

For dumplings:

1 egg	*4 tablespoons flour*
2 tablespoons water	*Salt to taste*

Melt butter in soup pot. Add flour, mushrooms and onions, and brown. Add paprika and water. Bring to slow boil. Make dumplings by mixing all ingredients together. Drop by the teaspoonful into the boiling soup. Cook for 5 minutes.

BEGINNINGS

Steadiness

Dishonest money dwindles away, but he who gathers money little by little makes it grow.

Prov. 15:11

In life a financial killing is rare. We don't all win the lottery. If you steadily earn each day and invest wisely, your money will grow with your work. Keep steady, stay on course, stay close to God: inevitably, you'll grow.

BEGINNINGS

Steady Cheddy Cheese Balls

2 *cups flour, sifted*

1/4 *teaspoon salt*

l/4 *teaspoon paprika*

1/2 *cup butter*

6 *ounces sharp cheddar*

cheese, grated

1/2 *cup water*

1 *large can olives of*

choice

Sift first three ingredients. Cut in butter. Add cheese and mix well. Add enough water to hold mixture together. Form balls around olives, and bake at 400° for 15 minutes.

BEGINNINGS

Listen

But whoever listens to me will live in safety

and be at ease, without fear of harm.

Prov. 1:55

When you talk to God, can you hear his answer? By having faith in him you will hear. Listening to other people is very important in daily life, too. Many times, when people talk to us, we just don't hear them. We don't really try to understand what they are saying. We may hear the words, but we don't go that next step of listening for what their words mean. Try to listen as God does.

BEGINNINGS

We Hear You Cucumber Salad

3 cucumbers

1/2 teaspoons salt

1/8 teaspoon pepper

3 tablespoons onion,

*   minced*

1 cup sour cream

2 tablespoons lemon juice

Peel and slice cucumbers. Sprinkle with salt, pepper and onion. Stir in sour cream and lemon juice. Chill until serving time.

MIDDLES

MIDDLES

Idle Talking

All hard work brings a profit, but mere talk
leads only to poverty.

Prov. 14:25

"Put your money where your mouth is." We've all heard that. All talk, no action people wear out their wits and their welcome with schemes that never materialize. Don't flap your mouth in the breeze. You have a dream. Take it to heart. Roll up your sleeves and get to work. Real effort pays off. Don't procrastinate. Do it now. You'll see good things happen.

MIDDLES

Action Chicken Casserole

2 large, chicken breasts,
   cooked and diced

1 can cream of chicken
   soup

3/4 cup sour cream

1 cup cooked rice

1 cup celery, diced and
   parboiled

1 teaspoon onion, grated

1 tablespoon lemon juice

1/2 teaspoon salt

1/2 cup cashew nuts,
   chopped

3/4 cup bread crumbs
   or Corn Flake crumbs

Mix chicken, soup, sour cream, rice, celery, onion, lemon juice and salt. Put mixture in buttered casserole and refrigerate for 50 minutes. Then place casserole in preheated oven at 550° for 1 hour. Top -with cashews and Corn Flakes. Since this recipe makes only four servings, you may want to double it.

MIDDLES

Serenity

Cast all your anxiety on him because he cares for you.

1 Pet 5:7

We get nervous. It's a fact of life. Our world is tough to live in. But each time you start to feel the sweat form on your upper lip, or the back of your neck get hot, or the chills begin—remember, God will do the worrying for you. Give the problem to him. Immediately. Consciously. Focus on placing yourself in his hands. You'll feel better right away.

MIDDLES

Anxiety-Free Ribs

6 pounds spareribs

1 box seasoned croutons

Milk to moisten croutons

2 apples, peeled and
    chopped

$^3/4$ cup sugar

1 teaspoon cinnamon

1/8 teaspoon nutmeg

$^{1/2}$ cup raisins, finely
    chopped

Ask your butcher for a pair of three-pound ribs. They should match. Put them together so that they form a pocket in between. Lace one side. Combine remaining ingredients and stuff ribs. Finish lacing. Bake at 550° for 2 hours.

MIDDLES

Blind Faith

We live by faith, not by sight.

2 Cor. 5:7

Your eyes can deceive you. But if you have strong faith, you pay no attention to temptation. God wants you to live by that kind of faith. He instills it in us. Our task is to follow.

MIDDLES

Blindly Hot Chicken Salad

1 chicken, cooked and cut up	1/2 teaspoon salt
2 cups celery, diced	2 tablespoons lemon juice
1 cup almonds, blanched	1 cup potato chips
1 cup mayonnaise	2 cups cheddar cheese, grated
	Dash of paprika

Mix first seven ingredients and put in casserole. Top with crushed potato chips, grated cheddar cheese and paprika. Bake at 350° for 30 minutes. Do not overbake.

MIDDLES

Celebration

"Bring the calf we have been fattening, and kill it; we are going to have a feast, a celebration, because this son of mine was dead and has come back to life; he was lost and is found." And they began to celebrate.

Luke 15:25

Celebrate each day as a gift. You are a lucky, chosen person. Don't forget that. Reflect on all the good in your life. Relish it! Today, push away each bad thought as it tries to spoil your special existence.

MIDDLES

Celebrative Lamb Medley

1 large onion, chopped	*1 cup couscous grain*
2 smashed garlic cloves	*1 1/2 cups water*
2 tablespoons olive oil	*2 tablespoons butter*
1 pound cubed lamb	*1/2 teaspoon salt*
1/4 teaspoon each	*1 cup sliced grapes*
coriander and mint	

In a saucepan saute onions and garlic in olive oil on low flame. Add cubed lamb and brown. Add coriander and mint, and cook, covered, for 25 minutes on low heat. Cook couscous in water, butter and salt. Take a mound of couscous and make an indentation in the center. Add the lamb mixture in center. Place a ring of sliced grapes around the outside.

MIDDLES

Compassion

The Lord will surely comfort Zion and will look with compassion on all her ruins; he will make her deserts like Eden, her wastelands like the garden of the Lord.

Isa. 51:5

As you walk about the world, look around you. Look at inanimate objects. Do they need repair? Open your heart and your senses. How do other people feel? Respect all creation. The well-being of all things is your well-being, too. Most of all, have compassion for yourself. Feel God's profound and tender care for you and all creatures.

MIDDLES

Compassionate Couscous

2 garlic cloves, chopped	*1 cup couscous*
1 onion, chopped	*1/2 cup nuts of choice*
1/4 cup olive oil	*1 cup dark raisins,*
1 ¼ cups water	*chopped*
1 teaspoon salt	*1//2 cups dates,*
1 cup parsley, chopped	*chopped*

In a separate pan, saute garlic and onions in olive oil. For couscous, in a medium saucepan combine water, two teaspoons olive oil, salt, and parsley. Bring to a boil and stir in couscous. Cover and remove from heat. Let stand 5 minutes. Fluff couscous with fork and add nuts, raisins, dates and the onion-garlic mixture. Return to heat for one minute, stirring vigorously.

MIDDLES

Confidence

In this way, love is made complete among us so that we will have confidence on the day of judgment, because in this world we are like him.

1 John 4:17

We all want to get to heaven. One day God will judge whether we are fit or not. It's a scary thought. But if we live as God wants us to, we will feel confident about heaven. God made us in his image, which means we can freely choose evil or good. Choosing God's will unites our spirit with his.

MIDDLES

Confident Easy Pot Roast

1 3- to 4-pound chuck   1 envelope mushroom
roast, 2" thick   gravy mix
                                                  1/2 cup red wine

Place meat in center of a large piece of aluminum foil. Sprinkle with gravy mix and pour wine over meat. Seal tightly. Bake at 550° for 2 to 5 hours.

MIDDLES

Discernment

Beware of false prophets who come to you disguised as sheep but underneath are ravenous wolves. You will be able to tell them by their fruits. Can people pick grapes from thorns, or figs from thistles? In the same way a sound tree produces good fruit but a rotten tree bad fruit. A sound tree cannot bear bad fruit, nor a rotten tree bear good fruit. Any tree that does not produce good fruit is cut down and thrown on the fire. I repeat, you will be able to tell them by their fruits.

Matt. 7:15-20

Observe carefully everything around you. You know the difference between good and evil. Fine-tune your senses to distinguish what helps from what harms. Through prayer and reflection, learn to rely on the inner wisdom God gives you.

MIDDLES

Discerning Fruited Meatballs

/ pound ground beef

1/4 cup chopped parsley

1/4 cup bread crumbs

1 garlic clove, crushed

1/2 teaspoon allspice

1 egg

1/4 cup cream

1/4 cup Parmesan
   cheese, grated

2 tablespoons flour

1/4 cup raisins

1/4 cup mulberries

1 onion

4 tablespoons olive oil
   for frying

2 tablespoons butter for
   frying

Mix all ingredients in bowl except onion. Saute onion lightly and add. Roll mixture into balls and fry until golden brown.

MIDDLES

Dreams vs. Fantasies

He who works his land will have abundant food, but he who chases fantasies lacks judgment.

Prov. 12:11

Distinguish between fantasies and dreams. Fantasies will never come true. They waste your time and keep you from working. Dreams become goals. Dream all you want. Let your mind roam free, thinking about what you can be and do. And keep working.

MIDDLES

Dreamy Ham Loaf

For ham loaf:

1 pound ground pork   *1 egg*

1 pound ground ham   *1 cup bread crumbs*

2 tablespoons-brown

   sugar

For broth:

1 cup brown sugar   *1/2 cup apple cider*

                   vinegar

Mix all ingredients for ham loaf together. Make broth.
Bake at 550° for 2 hours in broth, in loaf-size pan.

MIDDLES

Gifts of Love

Love is always patient and kind; it is never jealous; love is never boastful or conceited; it is never rude or selfish; it does not take offense, and is not resentful. Love takes no pleasure in other people's sins but delights in the truth; it is always ready to excuse, to trust, to hope, and to endure whatever comes.

1 Cor. 15:4-7

God gives us the spiritual gift of love. What a privilege it is to share this gift with others. When we learn from God how to love ourselves, people can feel the difference. Wherever we go, others sense the peace and joy we feel. You can't hide love. Share God's love all day.

MIDDLES

Dumplings of Love

Dumplings:

1 large head of cabbage

3 tablespoons butter

2 tablespoons honey

1 cup bouillon

Dash of salt

Filling:

1 pound ground lamb

1/2 cup rice

4 cups milk

1 tablespoon butter

Dash of salt

For dumpling shell, steam cabbage until leaves fall away easily. Mix filling ingredients together and fill cabbage leaves. Close each with a toothpick. Place cabbage dumplings in a casserole with 1 cup bouillon. Mix honey, butter and salt, and pour over dumplings. Bake at 550° for 45 minutes.

MIDDLES

Exultation

0 Lord, you are my God; I will exalt you and praise your name for in perfect faithfulness you have done marvelous things, things planned long ago.

Isa. 25:1

Shout God's name every day! If shouting out loud will embarrass you, think: "Yes, God! I'm yours. You are my joy." You'll feel better instantly.

MIDDLES

Exulted Macaroni Salad

4 cups cooked elbow
macaroni
1 cup ham or chicken,
cooked and diced
2 apples, cubed

3 tablespoons sweet
pickle relish
1/2 cup mayonnaise
Salt and pepper to taste

Mix all ingredients. Chill before serving.

MIDDLES

Flaming to the Tree of Life

And in front of the Garden of Eden he posted
the cherubs, and the flame of a flashing sword
to guard the way to the tree of life.

Gen. 3:24 -

In the Hebrew Bible the cherubim aren't babies, but winged monsters that guard God's throne. They stand at the entrance to the garden to limit how long people suffer the consequences of sin.

Protect your life and the ones you love with flames of integrity and passion. Believe with all your being. God gives you the mind to know and the heart to feel what is good, honest and true. Always fight for what's right.

MIDDLES

Flaming Filet Mignon

2 6-ounce steak filets	*1/8 teaspoon pepper*
1/4 cup cognac	*2 large shallots, minced*
1 tablespoon unsalted	*1/4 cup beef stock or*
butter	*canned beef broth*
1 tablespoon vegetable oil	

For steak:

Sprinkle steak with one tablespoon of cognac and let stand at room temperature for 45 minutes. In a heavy skillet, melt 1/2 tablespoon of butter in 1/2 tablespoon of oil. Rub the steaks on both sides with pepper. When the skillet is hot, add steaks, cover partially and cook over high heat until crust forms— about two minutes. Turn and cook the other side. Turn again to finish cooking.

For sauce:

Melt remaining butter and oil. Add the shallots and cook. Add remaining cognac. Ignite sauce with match and cook until flame burns out, about 50 seconds. Add beef stock; boil until liquid is reduced to 1/4 cup—2 to 5 minutes. Season with salt and pepper and pour sauce over steak.

MIDDLES

Giving

But just as you excel in everything— in faith, in speech, in knowledge, in complete earnestness and in your love for us—see that you also excel in this grace of giving.

2 Cor. 8:7

Don't work only on yourself and your virtues. God's work also includes giving to other people. We have talents that God has given us so that we can use them to bless others. Some might have less than we do. Others might benefit from our gifts though neither we nor they realize we're giving. When we can give and receive without thinking, we become part of God's grand design for humanity.

MIDDLES

Gifted Pot Roast

*4 to 5 pounds fresh beef
   brisket*

2 cloves garlic, chopped

1/2 teaspoon paprika

Salt and pepper to taste

4 carrots, sliced

*2 large onions,
   chopped*

In a heavy iron pot, brown the brisket very well on all sides for 1 hour. Do not cover. Do not add fat or water. Make sure the meat doesn't burn. Remove from the pot, retaining the juices, and slice against the grain in 1/4" slices. Sprinkle with fresh chopped garlic, paprika, salt and pepper to taste. Return to pot. Add carrots and onions, cut into small pieces. Cover and simmer about 3 hours. Make this a day ahead.

MIDDLES

Glory

If I were to seek my own glory that would be no glory at all; my glory is conferred by the Father.

John 8:54

You don't need to talk grandly about yourself. Glory belongs to God. If you follow his teachings, others will see God at work in you and give glory to God. Concentrate on doing good and the glory that belongs to you will come automatically.

MIDDLES

Glorious Shish Kebabs

1/2 *cup olive oil*

1/2 *teaspoon honey*

2 *pounds beef, cubed in*

   large chunks

1 *large package dates*

1 *large can black*

   pitted olives

2 *large onions,*

   quartered

1 *large, can green*

   pitted olives

Mix olive oil and honey in a small bowl. Alternate each remaining ingredient on a skewer, and brush with mixture of olive oil and honey. Broil approximately 5 minutes on each side.

MIDDLES

Glory of God

*So whether you eat or drink or whatever you
do, do it for the glory of God.*

1 Cor. 10:51

The glory of God is the greatest thing in the world.
Healthy eating and drinking habits that give the body
strength and beauty glorify the one who created the
body. Living for justice, peace and love exalts the
author of life. The glory of God in all its goodness is
golden and joyous, giving zest and energy to our days.
Love God and live for Him.

MIDDLES

Glory of God Brisket

6 pound brisket

Salt and pepper to taste

Paprika

6 onions

4 tablespoons chicken

fat

Water

Season the brisket generously with salt, pepper and paprika. Chop onions and saute them in chicken fat. Put brisket in a roasting pan, fat side down •with onions on top. Add one inch of water. Cover tightly and roast for 5 hours. Carve against the grain.

MIDDLES

Joyful God

Oh come, let us sing to the Lord! Let us shout joyfully to the Rock of our salvation.

Ps. 95:1

Sometimes when we get so tense, we forget some of these things that God asks us to do. He wants us to be joyful. He wants music and celebration. Right now, go turn on your radio, put any music you want on, go to your ipod and find a recording you like. Turn it on and blast it to the hills! Sing along, feel the sounds of God go through you and uplift you. If you don't have a radio or a ipod then do something even better. SING! Just let it flow through you and have the time of your life. Clap your hands and go for it.

Feel the Spirit! Feel the pulse of the music! Have the time of your life!

MIDDLES

God's Joyful Chicken

4 boneless chicken breasts	*1 cup pomegranate juice and pulp*
1/2 cup oil	*1 teaspoon honey*
1 tablespoon ground fresh mint	*1 teaspoon salt*
	1 tablespoon ground almonds

Marinate chicken for 1 hour in refrigerator in a bowl filled with all ingredients except ground almonds. Roll each breast in ground almonds and place on buttered cookie sheet. Drizzle remaining liquid over each breast and cook in 550° oven for 50 to 60 minutes.

MIDDLES

Good Things

Good things were created from the beginning for good men, as evils were for sinners. The prime needs of mankind for living are water and fire, iron and salt, wheat flour, milk and honey, the juice of the grape, oil and clothing.

Sir. 39:25-26

Savor all the good things. Wake up each day and realize that every single positive thing you are experiencing, either material or spiritual, comes from God. Don't be tempted by evil. Sometimes it really appeals to you. But God helps you tell the difference between good and evil. You know that in your heart. Trust God. Believe in yourself. Then you will always surround yourself with what is best for you.

MIDDLES

Good Things Casserole

2 garlic cloves, pressed

2 onions, chopped

1 tablespoon butter

4 cups chicken breast
   meat, cubed

1 teaspoon cumin

2 cans creamed corn

1 cup cheddar cheese,
   shredded

1 cup kidney beans

3 tablespoons butter

3 tablespoons flour

1/2 cup bread crumbs

Saute garlic and onions in butter. Add garlic, onions, chicken, cumin, corn, cheese and beans to greased casserole dish. Cream butter and flour together and drop in casserole. Stir. Spread bread crumbs over the top and bake at 550° for 1 hour.

MIDDLES

Hard Work

The sluggard craves and gets nothing, but the desires of the diligent are fully satisfied.

Prov. 15:4

Invest your energy to bring the best return. Choose wisely. Although God is guiding you, He trusts you to make good decisions. Thinking you can waste time is a mistake. Do that often, and you will starve—physically, emotionally and spiritually.

MIDDLES

Hard-Working Meatballs

2 pounds ground round

1 egg

1/2 cup bread crumbs

Salt and pepper to taste

1 cup onion, minced

1 1/2 cups sliced

   mushrooms

2 tablespoons butter,

   melted

1 cup beef broth

2 cups sour cream

l 1/2 tablespoons flour

1 teaspoon salt

3/4 cup caraway seeds

Nutmeg to taste

1/4 cup parsley

Noodles or rice, cooked

Combine ground round, egg, bread crumbs, salt and pepper. Shape mixture into bite-size meatballs. Brown, remove and drain. To drippings add onion, mushrooms and butter. Brown until most of the liquid evaporates. Add meatballs and one cup beef broth. Cook over low heat for 50 minutes. Blend together sour cream, flour, salt, caraway seeds and nutmeg. Remove meatballs from heat. Stir in sour cream mixture. Return to heat until heated through, but do not boil. Sprinkle with parsley before serving over noodles or rice.

MIDDLES

Hope

"The days are coming," declares the Lord, "when the reaper will be overtaken by the plowman and the planter be the one treading grapes. New wine will drip from the mountains and flow from all the hills."

Amos 9:15

If we believe in God, we always have hope. There can be moments of deep despair when we suffer a loss. Or little annoying things build up in a day and we think we're going to lose it. But if we take time, maybe just a minute, we can focus on all that God has given us. Remembering he has a plan for us, and that will be best, we will sustain that hope. Don't ever give up on God, for he never gives up on us.

MIDDLES

Hopeful Chicken

4 chicken breasts,	*1/4 cup butter*
boned and skinned	*1/4 cup water*
4 tablespoons flour	*1/4 cup white wine*
Salt and pepper to taste	*Juice of one lemon*
1/4 cup olive oil	*1 lemon*

Pound the chicken breasts until they are not thick. Make a mixture of flour, salt and pepper. Dredge the chicken in flour mixture. In a skillet add two tablespoons of olive oil and two tablespoons of butter. Place two breasts in pan and saute for 5 minutes on each side. Set aside in a glass casserole, and preheat oven to 550°. Cook the remaining breasts and place in casserole. Do not rinse out skillet. Add a little more olive oil, butter, water, wine and lemon juice. Scrape bottom with wooden spoon and keep stirring this gravy mixture for 5 minutes. Pour mixture over breasts. Slice remaining lemon and place slices hi between the breasts. Place covered casserole in oven and bake for 40 minutes.

MIDDLES

Humility

He humbled you, causing you to hunger and then feeding you with manna, which neither you nor your fathers had known, to teach you that man does not live on bread alone but on every word that comes from the mouth of the Lord.

Deut. 8:3

The very famous saying, "Man does not live on bread alone," makes so much sense. One must lead a fulfilled life; heighten your senses and feelings. Smell, taste, sight, sound, touch-—nourish them all. Listen to beautiful music, read good books, think spiritual thoughts. Nourish your spirit as well as your body. Being humble and aware, you will be filled.

MIDDLES

Humble Salmon Croquettes

2 pounds canned salmon   3 eggs

1 cup potatoes, mashed   1 small onion, diced

Salt to taste

Salted matzo meal

Drain salmon and place in bowl. Add potatoes, eggs, onion and salt. Add matzo meal to thicken enough for patties. Make patties, roll in matzo meal and deep fry until brown and crisp.

MIDDLES

Beginning

God blessed them and said to them, "Be fruitful and increase in number; fill the earth and subdue it. Rule over the fish of the sea and the birds of the air and over every living creature that moves on the ground."

Gen. 1:18

So it was in the beginning. God created everything in his own special way. He made all things in order, and creation works according to a divine plan. When you create something or begin anew, don't hesitate. By being creative you take part in the creative power of God. You can accomplish what you set out to do.

MIDDLES

In the Beginning Chicken

1 3-pound fryer chicken,	*1 1/2 cups*
cut up	*onion chopped*
3 tablespoons flour	*1 cup boiling water*
1 teaspoon salt	*1 tablespoon paprika*
1/4 teaspoon pepper	
2 tablespoons rendered	
chicken fat, warmed	
until liquid	

Dredge chicken pieces in mixture of flour, salt and pepper. Fry in fat until brown. Remove chicken and place in two-quart casserole. Set aside. Fry onions in the same pan. Spread onions over chicken. Pour water into frying pan. Add paprika. Bring to a boil. Scrape bottom of pan to make a thin gravy. Pour over the chicken and cover. Bake at 550° for 1 hour or until tender.

Alternate method: Simmer chicken on top of stove for 1 1/2 hours.

MIDDLES

Strength

Go and enjoy choice food and sweet drinks, and send some to those who have nothing prepared. This day is sacred to our Lord. Do not grieve, for the joy of the Lord is your strength.

Neh. 8:10

If you simply go about your business, the will of God will sustain you. Just as water glides in a stream, so your belief in God will give you the strength to carry on to success.

Don't let your boss intimidate you; don't let your love partner treat you with disrespect. You have the strength to stand up and be honorable. Like water flowing forward gracefully, live, with strength knowing God is guiding you all the way.

MIDDLES

Iron Strength Liver Stroganoff

1 pound chicken livers   *1 cup sour cream*

2 tablespoons chicken fat   *2 tablespoons sherry wine*

1 package onion soup   *Noodles or rice*
  mix

In a skillet, fry livers in chicken fat until done. In a separate bowl, mix the soup, cream and wine. Add to liver and simmer about 5 minutes. Do not overcook and curdle the cream. Serve over buttered noodles or rice.

MIDDLES

Joy

So I recommend the enjoyment of life, because nothing is better for a man under the sun than to eat and drink and be glad. Then joy will accompany him in his work all the days of the life God has given him under the sun.

Eccles. 8:15

When things start to trouble you, stop yourself. Relax. Take some deep breaths. Exhale slowly, and picture your troubles floating away. Find your center, where you feel contentment deeply. Take pleasure in simple things, such as dinner with family or friends. Nourish your spirit with gentle thoughts and people you love. Share your favorite meal with, your favorite folks.

MIDDLES

Joyful Lamb Stew

1 pound lamb, cubed in
   large chunks
1 tablespoon flour
2 tablespoons olive oil
1 onion
2 leeks
1 clove garlic

6 cups water
1 cup white wine
1 tablespoon dill weed
Salt and pepper to taste
2 large cucumbers,
   chopped
2 cups bulgur wheat
2 tablespoons butter

Dredge lamb in flour and brown in olive oil. Transfer to roasting pan. Add olive oil to pan and saute onion, leeks and garlic. Transfer to roasting pan. Add water, wine, dill weed, salt, pepper and cucumbers to roasting pan. Place covered in oven at 550°. Saute bulgur wheat in butter. Add to roasting pan. Stir, cover and cook for 2 to 5 hours at 525°.

MIDDLES

Judging

For by the grace given to me I say to every one of you: Do not think of yourself more highly than you ought, but rather think of yourself in sober judgment, in accordance with the measure of faith God has given you.

Rom. 12:5

A healthy yourself and ego is essential. You must believe in your abilities. But never overinflate your opinion of yourself. Conceit is dangerous and can impact your life very negatively. Judge yourself appropriately, as God does.

MIDDLES

Judgment Beef Casserole

3 to 4 pounds ground
    chuck
4 carrots, cut up
1 1/2 cups celery,
    chopped
3 to 4 onions, sliced
1 cup beef stock
2 cloves garlic

4 tablespoons minute
    tapioca
1 tablespoon sugar
1 cup Burgundy wine
2 cups chopped
    mushrooms

Combine all ingredients except mushrooms in a large casserole. Cover and cook at 250° for 5 hours. During the last 45 minutes, add mushrooms. Serve over buttered noodles.

MIDDLES

Mercy and Love

Hatred stirs up dissension, but love covers over all wrongs.

Prov. 10:12

Cherish the qualities of mercy and love. Hate doesn't help you. It tears you up inside and cuts you off from others. When you feel hate, take some deep breaths. Fill your lungs with fresh air and your heart with love, forgiveness and mercy. As you exhale, breathe out the toxic feelings of hate. When you focus on mercy and love, you draw others into your circle of love.

MIDDLES

Lovely Garlic Shrimp

3 cloves garlic, minced	*4 tablespoons bread*
1/3 cup olive oil	*crumbs*
2 tablespoons	*1 tablespoon dried*
peanut oil	*parsley*
1/8 teaspoon salt	*1 pound medium Gulf*
	shrimp

Saute garlic in olive and peanut oils for 4 minutes. Add salt, bread crumbs and parsley. Cook for 1 more minute. Add shelled and deveined shrimp. Cook until pink, about 2 minutes, then turn and cook 2 minutes on the other side. Serve with bread crumb-parsley topping.

MIDDLES

Nighttime

/ will praise the Lord, who counsels me; even at night my heart instructs me.

Ps. 16:7

While you sleep, God watches over you. He may speak to you through your dreams. Your heart pumps slowly, keeping your body functioning. Through the mystery of unconscious awareness, your brain continues to monitor the world. You wake up every morning, your body refreshed, your mind renewed. Sleep well, knowing your being and you are always in God's care.

MIDDLES

Midnight Mediterranean Pilaf

1/4 *cup butter*	*1 cup uncooked rice*
1 small onion, chopped	*1 can beef consomme,*
1/2 cup green pepper,	*1/2 cup water*
chopped	*Dash pepper*

Melt butter in a skillet. Add onion, green pepper, and rice. Brown for 6 minutes. Add remaining ingredients, cover and simmer for 50 minutes until liquid is gone.

MIDDLES

Doubt

But when Peter saw the wind, he was afraid and, beginning to sink, cried out, "Lord, save me!"

Immediately Jesus reached out his hand and caught him. "You of little faith," he said, "why did you doubt?"

Matt. 14:50-51

Always keep your faith in God strong. Without faith you become weak— easy prey for evil. Trust God's wisdom, even when doubts come. Pray every day; ask God to give you faith. By doing so you will grow stronger.

MIDDLES

Never Doubt Corn Ring

1 cup bread crumbs

4 tablespoons butter

1 1-pound can corn

2 eggs

1 can cream of

mushroom soup

1/4 teaspoon salt

1/4 teaspoon pepper

1/4 cup onion, chopped

1 cup green beans

Brown crumbs in butter; add all remaining ingredients except beans. Pour into greased ring mold.
Bake at 550° for 40 minutes or until firm. Heat beans
and pour into center.

MIDDLES

Obedience

All these blessings will come upon you and accompany you if you obey the Lord your God.

Deut. 28:2

Sometimes you may struggle to obey God's rules. But making the extra effort to follow his will really pays off. God created us for a reason, and gives us rules to live by for a reason. Regardless of how you feel you can do as God commands. Ask for help with specific problems. Expect an answer, and you will find it.

MIDDLES

Obedient Omelet

1 large green pepper,
   minced fine
1 tablespoon butter
2 to 3 eggs
Dash of milk

Salt and pepper to taste
2 teaspoons marjoram
1/4 cup sharp cheddar
   cheese, grated

Fry pepper in butter on low heat until golden brown. Beat two or three eggs in a bowl with a dash of milk, salt, pepper, and marjoram. Add sharp grated cheddar cheese. Pour mixture in pan with peppers and stir. Let it stand and continue to cook on low heat by pushing sides into middle gently, forming an omelet.

MIDDLES

Order

Thus says the Lord, who gives the light by day and the fixed order of the moon and the stars for light by night, who stirs up the sea so that its roar—the Lord of hosts is his name.

Jer. 31:55

Are you aware that God has created order in the world? Nothing happens by accident. The plant blooms in season; you get a new job just when God has ordained it. Look for God's design. Recognize the clues. Worry never changes God's plan. Don't try to force anything. Relax and believe.

MIDDLES

Orderly Potatoes

5 large baking potatoes	*Salt and pepper to*
1/4 cup olive oil	*taste*
2 large onions,	*1 tablespoon parsley*
chopped	

Preheat oven to 550°. Wash, the potatoes and cut them into small sections, keeping the skin on. Place them in a mixing bowl. Add olive oil, onions, salt, pepper and parsley. Mix thoroughly. Place on a cooking sheet or shallow baking dish and bake for 45 minutes. Potatoes should be crispy.

MIDDLES

Freedom

Now the Lord is the Spirit, and where the Spirit of the Lord is there is freedom.

2 Cor. 3:17

The power of God sets you free. When you believe, when you feel your faith deeply, you will open your heart and mind to the endless possibilities of life. Tap into that inner energy. Share it. Ignore negative thoughts. Realize you are never alone. God is with you, giving you freedom to be your own person and to live a productive life.

MIDDLES

Pasta "Free-tata"

8 ounces angel hair
    pasta, cooked
8 large eggs, beaten
4 large garlic cloves,
    minced
2 tablespoons olive oil
6 ounces soft goat cheese

2 tablespoons balsamic
    vinegar
1 cup frozen peas,
    thawed and cooked
3 tablespoons Parmesan
    cheese
1/4 cup basil, chopped

Preheat broiler. Combine angel hair, eggs and garlic in a mixing bowl. Season with salt and pepper. Heat 1 tablespoon oil in cast iron skillet. Add pasta mixture and spread evenly. Reduce heat to medium and cook 6 minutes. Cover and cook 4 minutes until the mixture is set. Transfer skillet to broiler and broil 5 minutes until top is golden. Sprinkle with goat cheese and broil 2 minutes more until cheese softens. Slide the "free-tata" onto a platter.

For topping:

Combine vinegar, 1 tablespoon oil, peas and basil. Season to taste. Top "free-tata" with the mixture, sprinkle with Parmesan cheese and serve.

MIDDLES

Negativity No More

Get rid of all bitterness, rage and anger, brawling and slander, along with every form of malice.

Eph. 4:31

Negative energy doesn't help anyone. It drags you down. When you dwell on bad thoughts, you crowd out thoughts that can heal, bless and energize. When you do something bad, you have lost the chance to accomplish something positive. Don't drag all the negativity around like so much dead weight. Turn yourself around this moment. Choose to do good.

Choose to be good.

MIDDLES

Positive Lamb Chops

6 shoulder lamb chops

1 can condensed

  consomme

1/2 cup celery, chopped

1/2 cup green onions

  and tops, chopped

1/2 teaspoon thyme

1 4-ounce can chopped

  mushrooms, drained

  (reserve liquid)

3 tablespoons flour

1 tablespoon parsley

  flakes

1 cup sour cream

Brown chops in small amount of hot fat. Sprinkle with salt and pepper. Drain off fat and add next four ingredients. Cover and simmer 50 to 45 minutes or until done. Move chops to one side. Stir mushroom liquid into flour and blend. Add slowly to consomme. Stir, cooking until thick. Add mushrooms and parsley flakes. Top chops with sour cream. Cover and heat 5 minutes.

MIDDLES

Rejoice

Though the fig tree does not blossom, and no fruit is on the vines; though the produce of the olive fails and the fields yield no mod; though the flock is cut off from the fold and there is no herd in the stalls, yet I will rejoice in the Lord; I will exult in the God of my salvation.

Hab. 5:17-18

Take a moment just to breathe. Breathe in God's goodness. Let your lungs expand and your muscles relax. As you breathe out, let your anxiety and hurry float into the atmosphere. God is greater than any material gift, stronger than any earthly obstacle. Rejoice in him. Close your eyes. Breathe in, breathe out, relax, rejoice ....again!

MIDDLES

Rejoicing Salmon from Habakkuk

3 tablespoons olive oil	*4 slices lemon*
2 tablespoons vinegar	*2 teaspoons dill*
4 salmon filets	*1 teaspoon honey*
4 slices yellow onion	*Dash of white wine*

Preheat oven to 550°. Mix oil and vinegar. Place each piece of fish on aluminum foil and sprinkle with oil and vinegar mixture. Place slice of onion and lemon on fish and sprinkle dill on top. Drizzle honey over it, add a little white wine and close up foil. Marinate fish in refrigerator for one hour. Bake fish for 55 minutes. Do not open foil. Fish will steam and be moist and juicy.

MIDDLES

Wake Up

Do not love sleep or you will grow up poor;
stay awake and you will have food to spare.

Prov. 20:13

Wake up. Get moving. Don't let the grass grow—
mow it and move! Keep working. Once you've done a
hard day's work, yu'll deserve time to play.

MIDDLES

Rise 'n' Shine Salmon Loaf

Small amount of oil	*1 egg*
3 medium potatoes,	*1/4 cup bread crumbs*
peeled and sliced	*1 can peas and carrots,*
1 large can salmon	*drained*
1 onion, grated	*2 tablespoons butter*

Grease bottom of baking dish with oil. Then line sides and bottom with thinly sliced potatoes. Mix salmon, onion, egg and bread crumbs. Pat into a loaf or oval shape and place in center of baking dish. Pour peas and carrots around salmon. Dot with butter. Cover and bake at 350° for 1 hour.

MIDDLES

Faith and More Faith

He replied, "Because you have so little faith.
I tell you the truth, if you have faith as small as
a mustard seed, you can say to this mountain,
'Move from here to there' and it will move.
Nothing will be impossible for you."

Matt. 17:20

Faith is what counts. Suppose you're frightened about something when you wake up. Say, "God bless this day. May I feel your strong love all day."

Or suppose you want to get off to a good start. Say, "Thank you, God, for a good night's sleep. I feel refreshed and energetic. Thank you for being at my side all day." When you believe God intends to do You good, you feel confident. It's easy to believe in yourself. Defeat each doubt as it comes along. Talk to God about it. Remember— this day can be exactly as God planned it, the best possible day.

MIDDLES

Salmon with Faith Mustard

4 salmon filets

Dijon mustard, to cover

1/4 *cup olive oil*

1/2 *cup seasoned bread*

crumbs

With your fist, pound each salmon filet between sheets of plastic wrap. Remove the wrap and spread mustard on both sides of the salmon. Heat a small amount of olive oil in a saucepan on high heat. Dip the fish in the seasoned bread crumbs and cook in the olive oil 2 to 5 minutes on each side, just enough to sear in the flavor.

MIDDLES

Satisfaction

The righteous eats to the satisfying of his soul,

but the stomach of the wicked shall be in want.

Prov. 15:25

Though temptations fill the world, they don't truly satisfy. True believers recognize them for what they are. Lust is nothing more than a fantasy. If you aren't righteous, you're starving spiritually. God, whom we worship every day, is our reality. He gives us good desires for love, peace and strong faith that nourish and satisfy. God intends for us to be satisfied. As you enjoy a well-cooked meal that nourishes your body, open your mind and heart to all that nourishes your soul as well.

MIDDLES

Satisfying Billed Pork

2 pounds cubed pork   *4 to 5 dill stalks*

cups bouillon 4 to 5   *Salt to taste*

parsley stalks

For sauce:

3 tablespoons butter   *1 teaspoon honey*

3 tablespoons wheat   *3 tablespoons finely cut*

  flour   *dill*

2 cups bouillon   *1 egg yolk*

2 tablespoons vinegar   *1 tablespoon milk*

In a large saucepan, cook pork in bouillon with parsley and dill stalks, and salt to taste; skim off fat, put aside. Brown butter and flour, and add bouillon from cooked pork with additional bouillon. Whip until smooth. Simmer for 5 minutes before adding vinegar, honey and cut dill. Add egg yolk for a zesty flavor; add a touch of milk to yolk for easy stirring.

MIDDLES

Seeking

And without faith it is impossible to please God, because anyone who comes to him must believe that he exists and that he rewards those who earnestly seek him.

Heb. 11:6

To get along in life you must have an inquisitive mind. Always want to learn more to seek knowledge and truth. Be a seeker. Keep searching out the best of everything, spiritual and material. Seeking in faith is its own reward, even before you find an answer.

MIDDLES

Seekers' Baked Chicken

8 to 10 boned chicken	*1/2 teaspoon pepper*
breasts	*1/4 teaspoon thyme*
3 tablespoons butter	*1/4 teaspoon rosemary*
3 tablespoons flour	*1 tablespoon chives,*
2 1/2 cups milk	*chopped*
1 teaspoon salt	*1 tablespoon parsley,*
	chopped

Brown chicken in butter in skillet. Place in casserole dish. Add flour to skillet, stirring thoroughly over low heat until mixture becomes dry paste. Add milk and other ingredients and cook until slightly thickened, stirring constantly. Pour over chicken, covering all. Bake in 525° oven for 40 minutes or until tender. Serve over rice. Serves eight to ten people.

MIDDLES

Armor of Faith

In addition to all this, take up the shield of faith, with which you can extinguish all the flaming arrows of the evil one.

Eph. 6:16

If you have unshakable faith, then it doesn't matter what people say or do. You can learn from constructive criticism and ignore cruel comments. You are a good person; with God's help you can handle anything. Never lose sight of that. When someone or something shakes you up, take a minute. Remember your faith. God will never let you down. Your faith is your shield.

MIDDLES

Shield of Faith Chicken

1 frying chicken, cut up	*1/2 cup butter*
1 teaspoon salt	*1/2 cup orange juice*
1 teaspoon pepper	*2/3 cup slivered almonds,*
1 teaspoon paprika	*toasted*

Wash chicken and pat dry. Combine salt, pepper and paprika, and rub into chicken until coated. Melt butter in pan with cover and saute chicken until golden brown on both sides. Cover and reduce heat. Cook 25 to 50 minutes, until tender. Remove chicken and keep warm in oven. Pour orange juice into the pan in which you cooked the chicken. Stir and cook over high heat until reduced by half. Pour over chicken and sprinkle with almonds. Serve with rice.

MIDDLES

Tests of Belief

Blessed is anyone who endures temptation. Such a one has stood the test and will receive the crown of life that the Lord has promised to those who Love him.

James 1:12

In times of testing, you often feel alone. But you aren't. God is watching over you, taking care of you, giving you knowledge, hoping you make the right decisions blessing you with his Spirit. You'll be stronger because you pass the test. When you live with respect and honor, as God teaches us, you receive so many blessings, it's impossible to receive them all. Count on God. He's always there for you.

MIDDLES

Tested Filet of Sole

8 thin pieces fresh filet
   of sole, washed and
   patted dry
Mayonnaise, to coat

Onion powder, to coat,
   about 1 teaspoon
Lemon wedges for
   garnish
Parsley for garnish

With a knife, spread a thin coat of mayonnaise over each side of the fish. Then sprinkle onion powder on one side. Lay the side with onion powder face up on a foil-covered broiler pan. Place in broiler with oven at 400° for 5 minutes. Garnish with lemon and parsley before serving.

MIDDLES

Truth-Finding

The stomach takes in all kinds of food, but some foods are better than others. As the palate discerns the flavor of game, so a shrewd man detects lying words.

Sir. 36:25-24

God gives us tools for living. Because we believe in Him and His teachings, we have the power to understand who or what is good for us. Not everyone always wants the best for us. Get such people out of your life. Listen carefully to what people say. Discern the truth.

MIDDLES

Truthful Game Hen Stuffed with Figs

1 cup figs	*1 large game hen or*
1/2 cup raisins	*chicken*
1/4 cup water	*1/4 cup honey*
1/2 onion	*³/4 cup chopped*
1/2 stick butter	*pistachios*
1/4 cup walnuts	

Cook figs and raisins in water. Pour off remaining water and save. Saute onion in butter and add to figs and raisins. Add nuts to this mixture. Stuff chicken with mixture. Mix honey with remaining water from fruit, pour over chicken and use for basting. Bake at 575° for 1 hour. Sprinkle with chopped pistachios and serve.

MIDDLES

Truth

God is spirit, and his worshippers must worship in spirit and in truth.

John 4:24

Every time you pray, deal in truth. Truthful thoughts and words, even those that are hard to face, come from God. Every time you think of him, every time you pray, be as truthful as you can with yourself and God. When we are truthful in spirit, in word and in deed, we will live good lives.

MIDDLES

Truthful Chicken, Olive and Nut Salad

1 whole chicken, boiled

1/2 cup (1 can) ripe
olives, chopped

1/2 cup shelled walnuts

Mayonnaise to taste

Pinch of sage

Salt and pepper to
taste

1 red pepper, thinly
sliced

Dice chicken, discarding skin and bones. Add olives and nuts. Moisten with mayonnaise to taste. Add sage, salt and pepper, and mix. Serve with sliced red peppers as garnish.

MIDDLES

Comfort

*Praise be to the God and Father of our Lord
Jesus Christ, the Father of compassion and the
God of all, who comforts us in all our troubles, so
that we can comfort those in any trouble with the
comfort we ourselves have received from God.*

2 Cor. 1:5-4

When I start to get upset, I try to stop and not panic.
Remembering that God is with me, I feel comforted. If
I focus on my faith and pray, I become calm and I can
cope. God's love is unconditional. He cares for me.

MIDDLES

Comforting Macaroni and Cheese

1 8-ounce package	*1 cup cheddar cheese,*
elbow macaroni	*shredded*
1/2 cup butter	*1 cup jack cheese,*
1/4 cup all-purpose flour	*shredded*
2 cups milk	*1 egg, beaten*
1 teaspoon salt	*Paprika*

Cook macaroni according to package directions, but don't add salt. Drain well and set aside. Melt butter in a saucepan over low heat, add flour and stir until smooth. Cook for one minute, stirring constantly. Gradually add milk, cooking over medium heat; stir constantly until thick and bubbling. Add salt and cheeses, stirring until melted. Gradually combine about 1/4 of the hot mixture with egg, and add back while continuing to stir. Fold cheese sauce into macaroni. Pour into a lightly greased casserole dish and sprinkle with paprika. Bake at 550° for 55 minutes.

MIDDLES

Wholeness

My son, pay attention to what I say; listen closely to my words. Do not let them out of your sight, keep them within your heart; for they are life to those who find them and health to a man's whole body.

Prov. 4:20-22

The power of God makes me whole. In his power I am a new creation, a whole new person, every day. I live each day to the fullest and greet everything around me with new joy. If I awake with unhappy thoughts or pain, I concentrate on being reborn. I am a free individual with great things ahead of her. I will feel better today.

MIDDLES

Wholeness Vegetable Casserole

2 onions, *sliced*	*1 fresh squash, chopped*
4 tablespoons vegetable oil	*1 pound potatoes, cubed*
	1/2 cup red wine
1 large eggplant, cubed	*³/4 cup vegetable stock*
1 package frozen green beans	*1/4 teaspoon sugar Salt and pepper to taste*
1 package frozen kidney beans	*2 tablespoons fine herbs, chopped*
2 pounds mushrooms, chopped	

Preheat oven to 550°. Saute onions in oil; add eggplant. Boil frozen vegetables in water to thaw. In an oiled baking dish, combine all vegetables with red wine, stock, sugar and spices. Stir thoroughly. Cover and bake for 1 hour, stirring occasionally. Add water if needed.

ENDINGS

ENDINGS

Belief

If any of you lacks wisdom, he should ask God, who gives generously to all without finding fault, and it will be given to him. But when he asks, he must believe and not doubt, because he who doubts is like a wave of the sea, blown and tossed by the wind.

James 1:5-6

Each day we face tests of our belief. If we stay strong and pure, we will pass unharmed by evil. Overcoming temptation provides evidence that we are saved. Take the challenges of life one day at a time. Relax. Your belief in God brings strength and goodness into your life.

ENDINGS

Believable Bread Pudding

6 tablespoons butter	*3 eggs*
3 tablespoons honey	*1 tablespoon grape juice*
10 slices bread	*1 1/2 cups cream*
30 almonds, grated	*Dash of cinnamon*
5 bitter almonds,	*1 cup berries of your*
grated	*choice*

Spread two tablespoons of butter and 5 table-spoons honey in baking dish. Butter bread and place in dish with grated almonds. Mix eggs, grape juice and cream, and pour over bread. Put a dash of cinnamon on top. Let stand for an hour before baking at 550° for 45 minutes. Serve with berries and cream on top if you wish.

ENDINGS

Contentment

But if we have food and clothing, we will be content with that.

1 Tim. 6:8

God did not create all things to leave us wanting. He provides us with the basic necessities of life. Through our faith, if we follow him, he gives us the tools to live well. Knowing that, we can be content and not eaten up with worry. We can go through our life feeling calm within. Contentment does not make us complacent. It gives us quiet faith and confidence, which allow us to do our best work and live life at its best.

ENDINGS

Contented Cookies

1/2 cup soft butter

1 cup flour

1/4 cup powdered
   sugar, sifted

2 eggs

1 cup sugar

3 tablespoons lemon
   juice

1/2 teaspoon grated lemon
   rind

1/2 teaspoon baking
   powder

1/2 teaspoon salt

Cut butter into flour and powdered sugar in a bowl. Spread evenly on the bottom of a greased 9" pan to form the base crust. Bake at 550° for 20 minutes.

For cookie batter:

In a bowl mix eggs, sugar, lemon juice, lemon rind, baking powder and salt. Use a blender if you wish. Pour mixture into baked crust. Bake at 550° for 20 minutes or until top feels dry. Cut into 1" squares while warm. Dust with additional powdered sugar.

ENDINGS

Diligence

The sluggard craves and gets nothing, but the desires of the diligent are fully satisfied.

Prov. 13:4

We must apply ourselves in life and make every effort to live up to the ideals God holds out for us. If we respect the path he has chosen and follow with wisdom and diligence, we will enjoy a good life.

ENDINGS

Diligent Shortbread

6 cups flour   *1 cup sugar*

1/2 teaspoon salt   *1 pound butter*

Combine flour and salt in bowl. Add sugar. With pastry blender or two knives, cut in butter. Blend well until mixture forms a dough. Cool in refrigerator for 1 hour to make dough easier to work with. Roll dough out 1/2" thick and cut into squares. Bake on ungreased cookie sheet at 500° for approximately 1 hour. Sprinkle with sugar and cool.

ENDINGS

Eternity

The world and its desires pass away, but
the man who does the will of God lives forever.

1 John 2:17

1 think how vast the universe is. Long before we were born, it existed. While we live on this earth, it swirls above and beyond us, seemingly infinite in its expanse. Long after we die, it will continue. Yet the work you do for God will never die. Like a circle widening on the still surface of a pond, it will live forever and, as a result, so will you.

ENDINGS

Eternal Cranberry Velvet

1 package raspberry	*1-pound can whole or*
Jell-0	*jellied cranberry sauce*
1 1/4 cups hot water	*1 cup sour cream*

Dissolve gelatin in hot water. Chill until slightly thickened. Fold in remaining ingredients. Pour into mold and refrigerate until set. Serve on salad greens.

ENDINGS

Conquering Fear

Have I not commanded you? Be strong and courageous. Do not be terrified; do not be discouraged, for the Lord your God will be with you wherever you go.

Josh. 1:9

God created the fear response. Fear kept ancient people alive—when they came face to face with a wild bear, they ran! Sometimes fears can control us, however. Believe in God, face what you're afraid of and overcome it. Knowing God is with you, rise above your fears.

ENDINGS

Fearless Scones

2 cups unbleached flour	1 egg
2 1/4 teaspoons baking powder	1/2 teaspoon salt
	1/2 cup mulberries
1/4 cup butter	1/4 cup whipped
2 tablespoons honey	cream

Mix all ingredients except mulberries and cream swiftly. Place individual spoonfuls on buttered and floured baking pan. Sprinkle with sifted flour on top and bake at 450° for 15 minutes. Serve with mulberries and whipped cream.

ENDINGS

Harmony

Above all, clothe yourselves with love, which
binds everything together in perfect harmony.

Col. 5:14

Harmony is at the heart of creation. At your best you are a harmony of body, mind and spirit. You nourish your body with good food. In the same way, nourish your mind with truth and wisdom, and your spirit with love and beauty. The harmony of body, mind and spirit resonates with the balance and unity of all creation. In a quiet time and place, find your inner peace. Breathe deeply, in and out. Listen for the harmony in the stillness of all things. Live out of that harmony all the time.

ENDINGS

Harmonious Apple Pudding

2 teaspoons chicken/at	*1 teaspoon cinnamon*
3 cups smashed matzo	*2 large eggs, slightly*
pieces	*beaten*
1/2 cup white raisins	*1/2 teaspoon salt*
3 tablespoons lemon juice	*4 apples, peeled and*
1/4 teaspoon grated	*sliced*
lemon rind	*1/4 cup sugar*

In a mixing bowl, combine warm chicken fat, matzo pieces, raisins, lemon juice, lemon rind, cinnamon, eggs and salt. Spread in a medium-sized buttered casserole. Add top layer of apples and dust with sugar. Bake at 550° for 35 minutes.

ENDINGS

Loving Others

And so we know and rely on the love God has for us. God is love. Whoever lives in love lives in God, and God in him.

1 John 4:16

God is love. It's that simple. Because God loves you, good things happen whether you deserve them or not. For example, there are all kinds of riches. Health is the greatest wealth in the world. What about kindness, sweetness or understanding? Picture God's love flowing to you and through you to everyone.

ENDINGS

Lovingly Baked Caramel Custard

For custard:

4 eggs	*1 teaspoon vanilla*
1/4 teaspoon sugar	*extract*
1/4 teaspoon salt	*1/4 cup granulated*
2 to 2 i/2 cups milk	*sugar*

Preheat oven to 500°. In a bowl, beat eggs with an electric mixer at medium speed until fluffy. Add sugar and salt. Beat until thick and lemon-colored. Add milk and vanilla, and continue beating until thoroughly combined. In a skillet over medium heat, melt 1/4 cup of granulated sugar, stirring constantly until caramel-like syrup forms. Immediately pour into six buttered custard cups. Pour custard through a fine strainer into cups. Set cups in shallow baking pan and place on an oven rack. Fill with hot water to ¾" from top of cups. Bake for 1 hour. Remove from oven and let cool on rack. Refrigerate until chilled. Unmold.

ENDINGS

Manual Labor

No longer will they build houses and others live in them, or plant and others eat. For as the days of a tree, so will be the days of my people; my chosen ones will long enjoy the works of their hands.

Isa. 65:22

You're more likely to succeed if you work hard. People who work skillfully with their hands have won honor throughout the ages. Doctors work with their hands; so do plumbers, writers and computer technicians. Be proud of yourself and what you do. Good honest labor contributes to the world and keeps food on the table. Keep up the good work!

ENDINGS

Laborer's Luscious Lemon

3 whole eggs

2 egg yolks

1/2 cup sugar

Rind of one lemon,

*   grated*

³/4 tablespoon

*   unflavored gelatin*

1/4 cup lemon juice

2 cups heavy cream

Ladyfingers, optional

Sweetened whole

*   strawberries, optional*

Beat eggs and yolks until lemon-colored and frothy. While beating, add the sugar in a slow stream. Continue to beat until thickened. Add grated lemon rind. Combine gelatin and lemon juice in heatproof measuring cup. Place in a double boiler and stir until dissolved. Add eggs to mixture. Beat well. In a separate bowl, whip cream until stiff. Fold gently into egg mixture. Pour over ladyfingers (if desired) in dessert bowl. Refrigerate 4 hours. Serve with sweetened whole strawberries.

ENDINGS

Perseverance

Let us not become weary in doing good, for at the proper time we will reap a harvest if we do not give up.

Gal. 6:9

I never give up. Giving up guarantees failure. Believe in God, be your best, work hard. Trust God for the results. You'll reap a rich harvest.

ENDINGS

Persevering Banana Muffins

1/2 cup butter	*1 1/2 cups flour*
1 cup sugar	*2 eggs, beaten*
1 cup ripe bananas,	*1 teaspoon baking soda*
mashed	*1/4 teaspoon vanilla*
4 tablespoons sour	*1/4 teaspoon salt*
cream	*1 cup walnuts or pecans*

Cream butter and sugar. Add mashed bananas and sour cream. Mix in remaining ingredients except nuts. Mix only until thoroughly moistened. Add nuts. Fill paper muffin cups 2/3 full. Bake at 550° for 25 to 50 minutes. Note: this recipe serves 15.

ENDINGS

Possibilities

Jesus said, "Everything is possible for him who believes."

Immediately the boy's father exclaimed, "I do believe; help me overcome my unbelief!"

Mark 9:23-24

If you believe, you can see that the world is full of possibilities. Dwelling on doubts makes it more likely that you can't achieve the success God wants for you. Believe in yourself; believe that God wants you to succeed. When you have negative thoughts, offer them to God. Ask God for courage to act on your positive thoughts instead. Every morning as you wake up, thank God for all the wonderful things you can do that day. Open your mind and your heart to all the possibilities.

ENDINGS

Possible Apple Crisp

4 cups apples, peeled and sliced	*1/4 cup butter*
1/2 cup water	*1 cup sugar*
1 teaspoon cinnamon	*3/4 cup flour*
	Vanilla ice cream, for topping

Turn apples into buttered casserole. Combine water and cinnamon, and pour over apples. Work butter, sugar and flour together until crumbly. Sprinkle over apples and bake at 575° for 35 to 45 minutes, or until top is golden and apples are done. Serve warm topped with ice cream.

ENDINGS

No Doubts, No Sin

All food is clean, but it is wrong for a man to eat anything that causes someone else to stumble. It is better not to eat meat or drink wine or to do anything else that will cause your brother to fall. So whatever you believe about these things keep between yourself and God. Blessed is the man who does not condemn himself by what he approves. But the man who has doubts is condemned if he eats, because his eating is not from faith; and everything that does not come from faith is sin.

Rom. 14:20-23

We love to eat! Eating gratifies us on so many levels: taste, smell, texture, comfort, excitement. Throughout the ages the people of God have received their food as a gift from God. Some observe special dietary practices to honor God; for example, some Jews eat only kosher foods and some Christians abstain from alcohol.

Enticing others to violate their conscience about what they eat is as sinful as gluttony. But receiving from the God we love the gift of foods we love is a double pleasure.

ENDINGS

Simply Sinful Chocolate Cake

/ package chocolate

cake mix

1 package instant

chocolate pudding

8 ounces sour cream

1/4 cup vegetable oil

1/4 cup water or

chocolate liqueur

4 eggs

Preheat oven to 550°. Grease and flour a Bundt cake pan. Place all the ingredients in a bowl and mix by hand or with an electric mixer. The batter shouldn't be perfectly smooth. Pour into pan and bake for approximately 45 minutes. At 40 minutes, stick in a toothpick. For a gooey cake, remove immediately; otherwise bake until toothpick comes out clean.

ENDINGS

Future

When I consider your heavens, the work of your fingers, the moon and the stars, which you have set in place.

Life unfolds in ever-changing cycles. One you may read to the teacher who taught you to read and who is now blind. The constantly shifting roles, the cycles of change, keep life exciting and fill the universe with endless fascination. The finger of God sets the cycles in motion.

ENDINGS

Sweet Potato Future Pie

2 large yams	*1/2 tablespoon*
1 1/2 cups sugar	*cinnamon*
1 cup evaporated milk	*1 1/2 tablespoons*
1 stick butter	*vanilla extract*
1 1/2tablespoons	*3 eggs*
banana or lemon	
extract	

Cook yams whole, then peel. Place in large mixing bowl. Cut yams crosswise. Add sugar, milk, butter, extracts and cinnamon. Mix into pudding consistency. Taste, and adjust flavor if needed. When satisfied, blend in eggs. Pour into pie shell. Bake at 575° to 400° for 1 hour.

ENDINGS

Worship

Worship the Lord, your God, and his blessing will be on your food and water. I will take away sickness from among you.

Exod. 25:25

Adore, honor and worship God every day. He blesses you and takes care of you every day. When you are well or sick or happy or sad-—God is always there. We are God's precious children.

ENDINGS

Worshipful Peach Pleasure

2 No. 2 (16-ounce) cans   *1 stick butter, melted*
   sliced peaches, drained
1 package yellow cake
   mix, dry

Place peaches in 9x14 cake pan. Sprinkle dry cake mix over peaches, then pour melted butter over cake mix. Place in 400° oven for 40 minutes.-Serve warm with ice cream or whipped cream.

ODDS & ENDS

ODDS & ENDS

Advice

Pride only breeds quarrels, but wisdom is found in those who take advice.

Prov. 13:10

Listen to the guidance of others, as long as they believe and follow God's teachings. Never stubbornly think that you always know best. Discussing your ideas and plans with people you trust will improve them. Most important of all, listen to the guidance of God.

ODDS & ENDS

Advisable Onions au Gratin

8 cups onion, chopped	1 teaspoon baking powder
1/2 cup water	1 teaspoon salt
3 1/2 cups cheddar	1/4 teaspoon pepper
cheese	4 tablespoons butter,
1 cup flour, sifted	melted

Cook the onions in water until tender — about 15 minutes. Drain well and put in mixing bowl. Add 5 cups of the cheese, plus flour, baking powder, salt, pepper and butter. Torn into a two-quart casserole. Sprinkle remaining cheese on top. Bake at 550° for 55 minutes or until browned on top.

ODDS & ENDS

Bow Down

Come let us bow down in worship, let us kneel before the Lord, our Maker.

Ps. 95:6

Take a moment each day to say hello to God. Nothing is more important. Say hello when you wake up in the morning. Put down your newspaper for a minute. Or take some time during the day. It only takes a second and it feels so good to know God is with you. Worship brings such contentment.

ODDS & ENDS

Bowing Down Party-Size Egg Salad

12 eggs

1 cup half-and-half

1/4 teaspoon paprika

Pinch of salt

Parsley for garnish

Hard boil eggs and chop them. Add remaining ingredients. Mix together. Garnish with parsley. Sprinkle additional paprika over the top.

ODDS & ENDS

Life Patterns

He makes springs pour water into the ravines; it flows between the mountains. They give water to all the beasts of the field; the wild donkeys quench their thirst. The birds of the air nest by the waters; they sing among the branches. He waters the mountains from his upper chambers; the earth is satisfied by the fruit of his work.

Ps. 104:10-15

As you go about your day, look around you. Savor the tastes and colors of the food on your plate. Notice how smooth or rough your clothes feel against your skin. Delight in the endless variation of plant and animal life. Take in the grandeur of sky, mountain and sea. Think of the cycle God uses to provide the water we need: snow, rain, river, lake. Water is life! Water makes everything grow. Stop what you're doing right now, and realize what a grand plan you're a part of. You're in God's hands.

ODDS & ENDS

Bread of Life

1 cup water	*2 large eggs*
1 package dry yeast	*2 tablespoons oil*
2 tablespoons sugar	*3 to 3 1/2 cups flour*
1 teaspoon salt	*1 large egg yolk*

Into a large mixing bowl, pour lukewarm water. Add each of the following one at a time and stir: yeast, sugar and salt. Add each and beat eggs and oil. Slowly stir in 5 cups of flour and mix. Place dough on floured board and knead 5 to 4 minutes. Add more flour while kneading if necessary. Dough should be elastic and not sticky. Place dough in large oiled bowl. Brush top of dough with oil and cover bowl with warm cloth.

Let dough rise 2 to 3 hours. Don't put bowl near an open window. After dough rises, put on floured board and pound out air with fists. Divide into four equal parts. Stretch and roll three of them until 1 ½" thick. Twist the three parts into a braid and place on cookie sheet. Divide the remaining quarter into three parts and braid. Place smaller braid on top of larger one. Brush with beaten egg yolk. Let sit 15 or 20 minutes. Bake at 550° for 1 hour.

ODDS & ENDS

Giving

Remember this: Whoever sows sparingly will also reap sparingly; and whoever sows generously will also reap generously. Each man should give what he has decided in his heart to give, not reluctantly or under compulsion, for God loves a cheerful giver.

2 Cor. 9:6-7

In life the principle of giving and receiving is very simple. You get back what you put in. Sow a little, reap a little. Sow a lot, reap a lot. You decide. God wants you to give joyfully and freely, not because you're forced to. Once you've tried it, you'll find giving and receiving surprises you with joy.

ODDS & ENDS

Cheerful Giving Bread

1 package dry yeast   *2 teaspoons salt*

1/2 cup lukewarm water   *1 teaspoon sugar*

1 cup lukewarm water   *4 to 5 cups flour*

Dissolve yeast in 1/2 cup water. Combine 1 cup water, salt and sugar. Add yeast liquid and flour until dough is stiff enough to handle. Knead on floured bread board until smooth and satiny. Cover and let rise, 1 1/2 hours. Divide in half. Knead and form into two long narrow loaves. Let loaves rise on greased baking sheet 50 to 60 minutes. With sharp knife make diagonal slashes across top. Bake at 425° for 20 minutes.

ODDS & ENDS

Craving

The Lord does not let the righteous go hungry
but he thwarts the craving of the wicked.

Prov. 10:5

Life can be very deceptive. We are tempted to crave many things. Wrong cravings can hurt us. But if we crave God's love and hunger for his wisdom, we will be rewarded. In your heart you know the difference between good cravings and bad. You can overcome hurtful cravings.

When you long for something harmful, focus instead on your hunger for God.

ODDS & ENDS

Cravable Potato Pancakes

4 large potatoes,	*1 egg*
grated	*1/2 teaspoon salt*
1 medium onion,	*2 tablespoons butter,*
grated	*melted*

Pour the grated potatoes and onions into a strainer to drain off excess water. Place in bowl, and mix in the egg and salt. Fry in butter over a slow heat, about 5 minutes on each side.

For a variation, use grated squash instead of potatoes.

ODDS & ENDS

Don't Despair

He who goes out weeping, carrying seed to sow, will return with songs of Joy, carrying sheaves with him.

Ps. 126:6

When things couldn't get worse, don't give up. Keep working. You will ultimately find joy in life. Let yourself experience difficult feelings like despair, but don't wallow in them. Move on. Don't let them paralyze you. Keep going forward. No matter how painful it is in the moment, in the long run you'll find good news.

ODDS & ENDS

Despair-Free Date Nut Bread

1 16-ounce box raisins	*5 cups flour*
1 16-ounce box	*1 1/2 cups sugar*
pitted dates	*4 or 5 eggs*
1 pound walnuts	*5 or 6 teaspoons baking*
3 cups boiling water,	*powder*
enough to cover	*1 or 2 teaspoons baking*
raisins, dates and	*soda*
walnuts	*2 teaspoons -vanilla*

Place raisins, dates and shelled walnuts in a large pot. Cover with boiling water and let set for 3 hours. Then, put remaining ingredients in the pot and stir. Use a tall pork and beans can, or the like. Butter the can using brown paper, and fill 2/5 full. Bake for 1 hour and 10 minutes at 325°. Remove from the oven and let cool in can. The top of the bread forms a mound and tastes like candy. Serve with cream cheese.

ODDS & ENDS

Reaping Energy

Let us not become weary in doing good, for at the proper time we will reap a harvest if we do not give up.

Gal. 6:9

Sometimes do you get so tired, you're almost in tears? If you're lucky, at times like that you might be free to rest for 15 minutes. Other times you can only escape briefly into a private area. Take some deep breaths. In spite of the weariness, you catch your second wind.

ODDS & ENDS

Energized Potatoes

6 medium potatoes, baked	*1/4 cup cheese of choice, grated*
1 cup sour cream	*Salt and pepper, to taste*
2 tablespoons chives	*3 tablespoons butter*
1 garlic clove, crushed	*Paprika*

Scoop potatoes out of shells and into shallow square baking dish. Mash fine with fork. Mix in all ingredients except butter and paprika. If too dry, add a little more sour cream. Dot with butter on top and more cheese. Sprinkle with paprika. Put under broiler until butter has browned. Serve immediately.

ODDS & ENDS

Faith

I pray that out of his glorious riches he may strengthen you with power through his Spirit in your inner being.

Eph. 5:16

God teaches us to have faith in our inner self, for he lives within us. What's on the outside can bother us only if we let it. Don't be afraid. Have faith. Shut your eyes and focus on your faith. Feel the warmth within. Know that God is with you. Complete faith overcomes sin, whether it comes from inside or outside.

ODDS & ENDS

Faithful Bread of Life

1 stick butter	*1/2 cup honey*
2 cups milk	*³/4 cup raisins*
5 pinches saffron	*5 to 6 cups flour*
1 packet yeast	*1 egg, lightly whipped*
1 egg	*³/4 cup almonds,*
1/2 teaspoon salt	*blanched and chopped*

Melt butter and pour into lukewarm milk. Add saffron and yeast. Add egg, salt, honey and raisins. Start working in flour. Let rise to double size. Knead dough again. Make into crosses by overlapping two pieces of rolled-out dough. Let rise again on cookie sheet. Brush with egg and sprinkle almonds on top. Bake at 525° for 1 hour.

ODDS & ENDS

Following

Carefully follow the terms of this covenant,
so that you may prosper in everything you do.

Deut. 29:9

Followers and leaders have equal value. Follow God's word faithfully. Others may watch how you behave. You may lead them without knowing it. Without faithful followers, no one can lead. Whether you lead or follow, do it proudly.

ODDS & ENDS

Followers' Pancakes

1 small carton (8-ounce)	*2 tablespoons flour*
sour cream	*1 teaspoon baking soda*
2 eggs	*1 tablespoon sugar*
1 teaspoon vanilla	

Mix ingredients together well. Fry in skillet or on griddle. Drop in silver-dollar-size amounts of batter. Turn when pancakes start to bubble. Serves two to three people.

ODDS & ENDS

The Cycle of Life

I tell you the truth, whoever hears my word and believes him who has sent me has eternal life and will not be condemned; he has crossed over from death to life.

John 5:24

Spirit never dies. Yet in all life there is death, and in death there is life. God weaves the two together in a cycle of light and darkness. As painful as grief may be, believe that beyond your pain waits inexpressible joy. Trust God's will. In the never-ending cycle of death and life, you will see your loves again.

ODDS & ENDS

Fruit of Life Bread

1 ½ cups unbleached
   flour
3 tablespoons butter,
   melted
1/2 cup ground barley
1 egg
1/2 cup honey

³/4 cup half-and-half
2 teaspoons baking
   powder
³/4 cup dates, cut
1 teaspoon salt
1/4 cup pistachios,
   chopped

Mix ingredients in large bowl and place in buttered bread pan. Bake for 40 minutes at 550°.

ODDS & ENDS

Gain

But godliness with contentment is great gain.

1 Tim. 6:6

How wonderful to feel comfortable and relaxed! We live in such a hassled world, we've got to remain calm just to survive. Trusting God can help us be tranquil and content. We work better, communicate better, and are better people when we rest in God's grace.

ODDS & ENDS

Gainful Potatoes

6 medium raw potatoes,
   grated
3 eggs, beaten
1 16-ounce carton
   sour cream

Salt to taste
6 slices bacon
1/2 cup onion, minced

Combine grated potatoes with eggs, sour cream and salt. Pour into well-oiled casserole. Cover with strips of bacon. Bake in moderate oven about 45 minutes, or until bacon is crisp and potatoes are done (they should be soft).

ODDS & ENDS

Gathering

He who gathers crops in summer is a wise son, but he who sleeps during harvest is a disgraceful son.

Prov. 10:5

Use your time efficiently. Even though a deadline seems far away, work on things early. Get your work done early. Never slack off during the busy season. Be responsible. Serve God with all your strength.

ODDS & ENDS

Gathering Eggplant

1 medium eggplant   Salt to taste

For batter:

1 cup flour, sifted   1 cup milk

1/2 teaspoon salt   1 tablespoon oil

1 egg, slightly beaten

Cut eggplant in half lengthwise; pare and slice 1/2" thick. Cut slices in 1/2" strips. Dip in batter. Fry in deep fat at 575° 2 to 5 minutes. Or fry in 1/2" fat 2 to 5 minutes, turning once. Sprinkle with salt and serve.

For batter:

Mix flour and salt. Combine egg, milk and oil. Add gradually to flour. Beat until smooth.

ODDS & ENDS

Generosity

Give and it will be given to you. A good measure, pressed down, shaken together and running over, will be poured into your lap. For with the measure you use, it will be measured to you.

Luke 6:58

Good cooks measure ingredients carefully. The best cooks, however, depend on their intuition, knowing from experience how much they need of herbs and spices to create tasty food. Giving is a key ingredient in a happy life. People who give wisely and gladly receive more than they give. Generous giving grows out of trusting God's abundance. You can give all you have joyfully because you know that God will supply all your needs according to his riches.

ODDS & ENDS

Generously Measured Polenta

4 cups water

1 teaspoon salt

1 cup polenta, a kind
   of corn meal

1 cup fresh corn kernels

Pat of unsalted butter

Fresh cheese of your
   choice, grated, for
   topping

In a saucepan bring water to boil, reduce heat to low and add salt. Slowly pour in the polenta, stirring constantly for 5 or 4 minutes until mixture is thicker. Add fresh corn. Reduce heat to low and cook for 35 minutes. If mixture gets too thick, add water. Serve with a pat of butter and grated cheese on top.

ODDS & ENDS

Grace

Grace to you and peace from God our Father.

1 Cor. 1:5

God's grace means mercy and kindness. God's peace means wholeness and harmony. Seventeen New Testament letters include the greeting "Grace and peace" in the first few verses. In our secular world, people say a refined, elegant person is graceful. Peace means the absence of conflict in the world or within ourselves. Make these essential ingredients of your daily life. Treat others with mercy and kindness, whether they are deserving or not. Bring abundant life and harmony of spirit to everyone around you.

ODDS & ENDS

Graceful Heaven Cakes

8 apples

1 cup crumbled dry

bread chunks

1 teaspoon cinnamon

1/2 cup honey

1 stick of butter

1/2 cup raisins

1/2 cup dates

For sauce:

2 eggs

1 1/2 cups cream

1 tablespoon butter

1 tablespoon flour

1 teaspoon sweet spices:

cinnamon, sugar,

nutmeg, etc.

Peel apples and cut into wedges. Place in buttered baking dish. Sprinkle with bread chunks and cinnamon, and swirl honey on top. Dot with butter and bake in oven at 575° for 40 minutes.

For sauce:

Beat eggs lightly and stir in cream. Place on low flame. Cream together butter and flour, and drop small dots into eggs and cream. Add spices. Chill and serve over warm heaven cake.

ODDS & ENDS

Harvesting

*The Lord will indeed give what is good, and
our land will yield its harvest.*

Ps. 85:12

Every day we benefit from God's bounty. Open
your eyes to God's goodness. Notice his blessings.
Nurture your awareness of his Spirit within you.
Respect the Spirit of God you meet in others. Live by
God's teachings. If you do these things, you will reap
a great harvest.

ODDS & ENDS

Harvest Corn Pie

*1 16-ounce can
   creamed corn
1/2 cup corn meal
2 tablespoons sugar or
   honey
1/2 cup milk*

*1 cup cheddar or cheese
   of choice, grated
Salt and pepper,
   cayenne preferred
3 tablespoons butter*

Grease a 9" pie pan. In a mixing bowl combine corn, corn meal, sugar, milk, half of cheese, salt, pepper and butter. Pour into the pie pan and sprinkle remaining cheese on top. Bake at 400° for 50 minutes.

ODDS & ENDS

Real Faith

Your kingdom come, your will be done on earth as it is in heaven.

Matt 6:10

God is always with me. I don't need to be afraid of insecurity or doubt. If I have questions or feel confused, I can pray. God will help me work through my problem. God showers me with his grace because I am one of his children. When he rules in my life as he rules in heaven, his kingdom comes to reality in me.

ODDS & ENDS

Real Faithful Green Rice

½ leek, chopped

1/2 green onion,

   chopped

2 tablespoons olive oil

1 tablespoon butter

3 cups chicken bouillon

3/4 cup rice

1/2 cup barley flakes

2 tablespoons parsley

Saute leek and onion in oil and butter. Add bouillon and washed rice. After cooking 10 minutes, add barley flakes and parsley. Cook, covered, 10 minutes more.

ODDS & ENDS

Mercy

Do not withhold your mercy from me, O Lord;

may your love and your truth always protect me.

Ps. 40:11

Nobody's perfect. In times of failure and struggle, we often beat up on ourselves. We feel as though God has forsaken us. Feelings often differ from facts. Your failures don't surprise God. Your struggles become His struggles, as you surrender all that you are to Him. Count on his mercy. Trust His love. Try again to be your best self. Forget how many times you fall; it doesn't matter as long as you get up one time more than you fall.

ODDS & ENDS

Merciful Knishes

1 egg, slightly beaten	*1/2 teaspoon baking*
1/3 to 1/2 cup water	*powder*
1 1/2 cups flour	*1/2 cup shortening*
	Salt to taste

For fillings:

Mashed potatoes	*Hoop cheese mixed with*
seasoned with	*egg, salt and sugar*
sauteed onions	*to taste*

To the beaten egg add enough water to make 1/2 cup liquid. Mix flour, baking powder, salt and shortening together as pie dough. Add the 1/2 cup liquid. Form into large ball. Separate into four easy-to-handle portions. Roll out each on a pastry board. Spread either filling on one side of dough. Roll up like a jelly roll and cut into 1 1/2" slices. Place on greased cookie sheet, cut side down. Bake at 375° for 55 minutes.

ODDS & ENDS

Freedom of Spirit

/ mean to deliver them out of the hands of Egyptians and bring them up out of that land to a land rich and broad, a land where milk and honey flow.

Exod. 55:5

Never allow anyone to rob you of your freedom of spirit. If someone around you doesn't treat you as you deserve, you are still free to show them the kindness God shows you. Or you have the freedom to let them go. Believe God wants the best for you. That's why you were born. Cherish the gift of freedom! You are very special!

ODDS & ENDS

Honeyed Apples of Freedom

4 apples, chopped

1/2 cup water

1/2 cup honey

1/2 pint fresh cream

Pinch of cinnamon

Pistachio nuts, chopped, as topping

Peel and halve apples, remove core. Cook in water and honey for 5 minutes. Let cool. Whip cream and serve with cinnamon and nuts.

ODDS & ENDS

True Riches

A faithful man will be richly blessed, but one eager to get rich will not go unpunished.

Prov. 28:20

Make sure you choose worthwhile goals. If you go after money or pleasure or other shallow things, you may get them. But they contain their own punishment. Far from satisfying, they leave you unfulfilled. God will provide you his riches, material and spiritual. Stay faithful.

ODDS & ENDS

Rich 'n' Spicy Cashew Nuts

1 1/2cups cashew nuts   *1/2 teaspoon onion salt*

2 tablespoons butter   *1/4 teaspoon garlic salt*

1 teaspoon celery salt

Brown nuts in butter. Drain on paper. Sprinkle seasonings over nuts. Yields 1 1/2 cups.

ODDS & ENDS

Reach Out

Then he said to Thomas, "Put your finger here; see my hands. Reach out your hand and put it into my side. Stop doubting and believe."

John 20:27

Some people believe only in things they can touch or see. They require proof. Thomas listened more to his doubts than to his faith. He demanded indisputable evidence. Faith can never be proved beyond doubt. Believe with your heart and your head. God keeps his word.

ODDS & ENDS

Reach Out Carrot Ring

1/2 cup vegetable
  shortening

1/2 cup brown sugar

1 egg

Juice of one lemon

1 cup flour

1/2 teaspoon baking
  soda

1 teaspoon baking
  powder

Salt to taste

1 1/2 cups raw carrots,
  grated

Cream shortening and sugar; add egg, lemon juice, flour, baking soda, baking powder, and a dash of salt. Mix thoroughly before adding carrots. Pour into a six-cup ring mold. Bake at 550° for 1 hour.

ODDS & ENDS

Reward

Great are your purposes and mighty are your deeds. Your eyes are open to all the ways of men; you reward everyone according to his conduct and as his deeds deserve.

Jer. 32:19

Someone is always assessing our character and actions, just as we form opinions about others. Most of the time, friends are people we like and approve of. We may not know consciously why we choose one person for a friend rather than another. Yet we can choose whomever we want. Good friends give us a moral and emotional lift. Decide wisely about who your friends are. Few things in life reward us more than a good friend.

ODDS & ENDS

Rewarding Easy Spinach

1 package frozen
   chopped spinach
1 tablespoon butter
1 tablespoon flour
1/2 cup sour cream

1/2 teaspoon onion,
   minced
1/4 teaspoon lemon juice
Salt and pepper to taste

Cook spinach according to package directions. Drain thoroughly and set aside. In a new saucepan melt butter. Blend in flour. Add sour cream, minced onion, lemon juice, salt and pepper. Stir constantly until mixture thickens slightly. Combine with spinach. Refrigerate. Before serving, reheat slowly.

ODDS & ENDS

Personal Care

Do you not know that your body is a temple
of the Holy Spirit, who is in you, whom you have
received from God?

1 Cor. 6:19

The body is the temple of God's Spirit. He wants us to take care of our physical self. Drink only the purest waters and juices. Eat wholesome grains, produce and meats, like those mentioned in the Bible. By taking care of our body, we honor our creator. He plans for us to live long healthy lives, and enjoy all the riches of creation.

ODDS & ENDS

Rice of Care

1 tablespoon butter	*³/4 cup rice, washed in*
1/4 cup millet	*water*
2 tablespoons olive oil	*Monterey Jack cheese,*
1 teaspoon allspice	*grated, for topping*
1/2 clove garlic, crushed	
1 cup water	

In a frying pan, melt butter and toast millet. In a saucepan, warm oil, add allspice and fry crushed garlic for a few seconds. Add water, washed rice and millet. Cover and cook for 20 minutes. Sprinkle with grated cheese before serving.

ODDS & ENDS

Righteousness

Sow for yourselves righteousness, reap the fruit of unfailing love, and break up your unplowed ground; for it is time to seek the Lord, until he comes and showers righteousness on you.

Hos. 10:12

God wants you to go for your dream. Sow, reap, work! Do it all for the sake of righteousness. You'll receive your reward. Eat, drink, live, love! Have confidence that God created the gifts of life and intends you to enjoy them.

ODDS & ENDS

Righteous Mint Relish

2 cups fresh mint leaves, packed

4 pounds tan apples, peeled and cored

4 large onions, peeled and chopped

2 large sweet red peppers chopped, seeded

1 1/2 cups raisins

3 cups white vinegar

1/2 cup water

4 cups sugar

2 teaspoons salt

2 tablespoons mustard seed

Chop mint leaves, apples, onions, peppers and raisins in the food processor, using a coarse blade. Combine vinegar, water, sugar, salt and mustard seed in a large kettle. Boil for 5 minutes. Add chopped ingredients. Return to boil for another 50 minutes, stirring often. Ladle into hot, sterilized canning jars and seal immediately. Makes 7 to 8 pints.

ODDS & ENDS

Wisdom

God said to Solomon, "Since this is your heart's desire and you have not asked for wealth, riches or honor, nor for the death of your enemies, and since you have not asked for a long life but for wisdom and knowledge . . . therefore wisdom and knowledge will be given to you."

2 Chron. 1:11-12

We have wisdom when we don't even know it. A strong belief in God's words will guide you all of your days. Never doubt your feelings inside. They are being given to you by him. Trust that, and wisdom will be yours.

If you believe, you will have all the riches God meant for you.

ODDS & ENDS

Solomon's Corn Bread

Liquid:

1 tablespoon honey

³/4 cup milk

1 egg

1 cob corn

3 tablespoons butter

Dry:

³/4 cup corn meal

1/2 cup wheat flour

1/2 teaspoon salt

*2 teaspoons double-
    acting baking
    powder*

Combine liquid ingredients. In a separate bowl combine dry ingredients. Pour liquid into the dry ingredients and combine with a few quick strokes. Cook corn for 5 minutes in salted water. Scrape kernels off with a knife and add to mixture. Pour into buttered baking dish and bake at 425° for 25 minutes.

ODDS & ENDS

Heart and Soul

Dear friend, I pray that you may enjoy good health and that all may go well with you, even as your soul is getting along well.

5 John 1:2

Isn't it wonderful to know that God is always with you? But sometimes, when life is going great, it's easy to forget to pray. Pray every day. Thank God for your health. Eat right.

ODDS & ENDS

Soulful Blintz Souffle

3 tablespoons butter

16 frozen blintzes

12 eggs

1 ½ pints sour cream

1 teaspoon vanilla

extract

1/3 cup sugar

Grease rectangular pan with butter. Place blintzes in one layer in pan. Blend all other ingredients and pour over blintzes. Refrigerate overnight. Bake at 550° uncovered for 45 minutes, until souffle rises and top is golden brown at the edges. Serves 8 to 10.

ODDS & ENDS

Success

Then you will have success if you are careful to observe the decrees and laws that the Lord gave Moses for Israel. Be strong and courageous. Do not be afraid or discouraged.

1 Chron. 22:15

If you follow the rules of life with courage and energy, you will achieve success. Following the rules honors God, who made them. God sees that all creation works as a whole. You have a unique place in God's plan. Go for it.

ODDS & ENDS

Successful Egg-Cheese Surprise

Butter, enough to
    butter bread
10 slices egg bread,
    crust removed
6 eggs

3 cups milk
1 package jack cheese,
    grated
1 package sharp
    cheddar cheese, grated

Butter bottom of bread slices. Blend eggs with milk. Place a layer of bread on bottom of pan. Layer jack and cheddar cheese over bread. Repeat until all bread is used. Pour egg mixture over bread and cheese layers. Refrigerate overnight. Bake at 350° for 1 hour.

ODDS & ENDS

Worry

Therefore I tell you, do not worry about your life, what you will eat or drink; or about your body, what you will wear. Is not life more important than food, and the body more important than clothes?

Matt. 6:25

Food, clothes and many other things do matter in life. But nothing else matters if you fail to live well in the eyes of God. If you are living properly, don't keep worrying about anything because God will take care of you. When you start to worry, take a minute and ask if you are doing something unwise or unhealthy. If you are, stop now and ask God to help you live in ways that will do you good. If you decide that you are living appropriately, relax. A habit of worrying will only make you nervous and keep you from getting a good night's sleep. God is watching out for us all. Take a deep breath. Remember how close to you God's Spirit is.

ODDS & ENDS

Worry-Free Applesauce Puffs

For puffs:

2 cups packaged	*1/2 cup applesauce*
biscuit mix	*1/4 cup milk*
1/4 cup sugar	*1 egg, slightly beaten*
1 teaspoon cinnamon	*2 tablespoons cooking oil*

Combine biscuit mix, sugar and cinnamon. Add applesauce, milk, egg and cooking oil. Beat vigorously for 30 seconds. Fill greased 2" muffin pans 2/3 full. Bake at 400° for 12 minutes or until golden. Cool slightly before removing from pans.

For topping:

1/4 cup sugar	*2 tablespoons butter,*
1/4 teaspoon cinnamon	*melted*

Mix sugar and cinnamon. Dip tops of muffins in butter and in the sugar-cinnamon mix. Makes 24 muffins.

LaVergne, TN USA
06 October 2010
199742LV00001B/68/P